REMARKABLE INSECTS

A photographic safari

Remarkable Insects

of South Africa

Lambert Smith

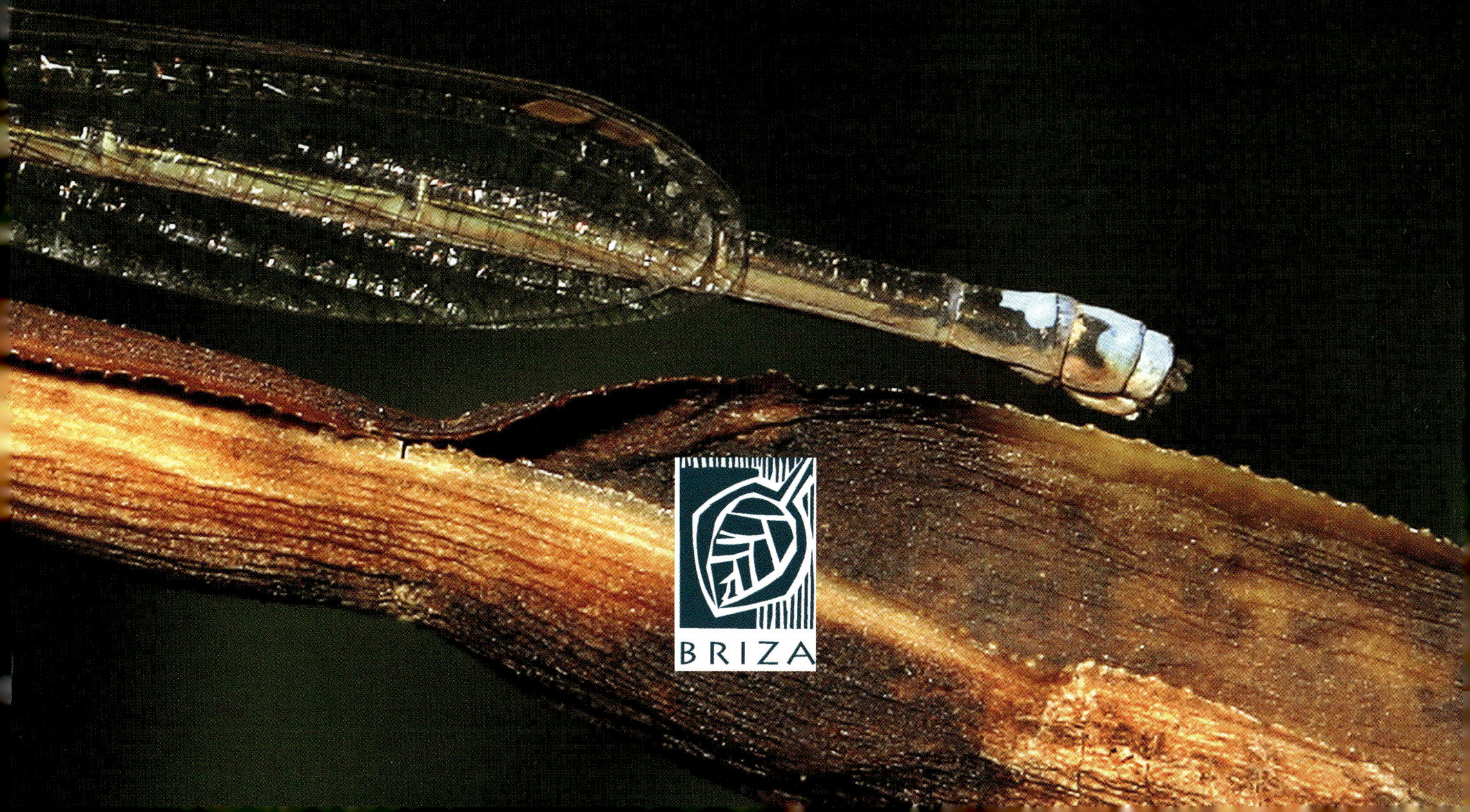

BRIZA

Published by
BRIZA PUBLICATIONS
CK 1990/11690/23

www.briza.co.za

PO Box 56569
Arcadia 0007
Pretoria
South Africa

First edition, first impression 2008

Copyright © in text: Lambert Smith
Copyright © in photographs: Lambert Smith
Copyright © in published edition: Briza
   Publications

All rights reserved. No part of this publication may be reproduced or transmitted in any form or by any means without written permission of the copyright holders.

ISBN 978 1 875093 43 4

Project manager: Reneé Ferreira
Cover design: Sally Whines
Inside design and typesetting: Alicia Arntzen, Purple Turtle Publishing Services
Printed and bound by Tien Wah Press (Pte.) Ltd, Singapore

Acknowledgements

I would like to extend my appreciation to the following organisations and individuals who have contributed in some way to make this book possible.

The management and staff of the National Botanical Garden in Pretoria and especially Karen Behr and Lynette Ferreira with whose kind permission and assistance I was able to move freely about the garden to take photographs. Dr John Anderson of SANBI who allowed me to photograph some of the valuable insect fossils in his care. Dr Rob Toms of the Transvaal Museum for his assistance with the Big 12 insects. Quinten and Ansophia Venter for their kind hospitality while we were taking insect photographs in the Hectorspruit area.

A special thanks to the many friends who eagerly searched for insects on their properties and carried them to me in an assortment of bottles, cans, boxes and other containers. In this respect I would especially like to mention Anton Hugo, Johan Olivier and family, Liezel Struwig and family, Sonja Ehlers, Jonathan, Jarred and Kendall Smith.

Finally a very special thank you to my wife Lorraine who enthusiastically joined in on my many insect spotting and photography expeditions and who endured having countless creepy-crawlies brought into the house.

Contents

Introduction...........10
- What is an insect?...........12
- The basics of insect anatomy...........13
- Metamorphosis...........15
- The role of insects...........16
- Insects from the past...........18

Flies...........20
Order Diptera...........20
- Robber Flies: Family Asilidae...........24
- Hover Flies: Family Syrphidae...........26
- Blow Flies: Family Calliphoridae...........29
- Fruit Flies: Family Tephritidae...........31
- Bee Flies: Family Bombyliidae...........32
- Flesh Flies: Family Sarcophagidae...........33
- Moth Flies: Family Psychodidae...........33
- Stalk-eyed Flies: Family Diopsidae...........34
- Tachinid Flies: Family Tachinidae...........34
- Mosquitoes: Family Culicidae...........35

True Bugs...........38
Order Hemiptera...........38
- Shield Bugs: Family Pentatomidae...........40
- Shield-backed Bugs: Family Scutelleridae...........43
- Assassin Bugs: Family Reduviidae...........44
- Aphids: Family Aphididae...........46
- Australian Bug: Family Margodidae...........47
- Twig Wilter Bugs: Family Coreidae...........48
- Treehoppers: Family Membracidae...........499
- Leafhoppers: Family Cicadellidae...........51
- Spittle Bugs: Family Cercopidae...........52
- Twig Snout Bugs: Family Fulgoridae...........53

Mantids...........54
Order Mantodea...........54

Ants, Bees and Wasps ... 60
Order Hymenoptera ... 60
Ants ... 63
Bees ... 66
Carpenter Bees: Subfamily Xylocopinae ... 68
Honey Bees: Family Apidae ... 69
Wasps ... 71
Paper Wasps: Family Vespidae ... 71
Potter Wasps: Subfamily Eumenidae ... 74
Mud Wasps and Sand Wasps: Family Sphecidae ... 76
Parasitic wasps ... 78

Butterflies and Moths ... 80
Order Lepidoptera ... 81
Butterflies ... 83
Swallowtails and Orange Dogs: Family Papilionidae ... 83
Garden Acraea: Family Nymphalidae ... 86
Sulphurs and Whites: Family Pieridae ... 87
Skippers: Family Hesperiidae ... 88
Yellow Pansy: Family Nymphalidae ... 89
Painted Lady: Family Nymphalidae ... 90
African Monarch: Family Nymphalidae ... 91
Coppers and Blues: Family Lycaenidae ... 92
Moths ... 93
Bagworms Moths: Family Psychidae ... 93
Owl Moths: Family Noctuidae ... 94
Plume Moths: Family Pterophoridae ... 94
Crimson-speckled Footman: Family Agaristidae ... 95
Hawk Moths: Family Sphingidae ... 96
Oleander Hawk Moth ... 96
African Humming Bird Moth ... 96
Clear-wing Moths: Family Sesiidae ... 96
Golden Plusia: Family Noctuidae ... 98
Fig-tree Moth: Family Lymantriidae ... 99
Caterpillars ... 99

Beetles 104
Order Coleoptera 104
Dung Beetles: Family Scarabaeidae 108
Long-horn Beetles: Family Cerambycidae 110
Ladybirds: Family Coccinellidae 112
Fruit Chafer Beetles: Subfamily Cetoniinae 117
Weevils: Family Curculionidae 119
Blister Beetles: Family Meloidae 120
Darkling Beetles: Family Tenebrionidae 121
Predacious Water Beetles: Family Dytiscidae 122
Net-winged Beetles: Family Lycidae 123
Ground Beetles: Family Carabidae 125

Lacewings and Antlions 126
Order Neuroptera 126
Lacewings: Family Chrysopidae 127
Antlions: Family Myrmeleontidae 129
Mantidflies: Family Mantispidae 133

Grasshoppers and Crickets 134
Order Orthoptera 134
Short-horned Grasshoppers: Family Acrididae 139
Wingless Grasshoppers: Family Lentulidae 143
Foam Grasshoppers: Family Pyrgomorphidae 143
Long-horned Crickets and Katydids........................145
King Cricket: Family Anostostomatidae..............145
Mole Cricket: Family Gryllotalpidae...................147
Katydids: Family Tettigoniidae 149

Dragonflies and Damselflies............152
Order Odonata..152
Dragonflies 154
Damselflies 157

Cockroaches..160
Order Blattodea..160

Termites 164
Order Isoptera 164

Mayflies 170
Order Ephemeroptera...170

Insect spotting 171
- What does insect spotting entail? 172
- The tools of the insect spotter 173
- Where to look for insects 174
- Seasonality and regional locality of insects 176
- South Africa's Big 12 177

Digital insect photography 181
- Insects as subjects 182
- Using digital cameras 183
- A question of mindset 184
- Train your brain 184
- Getting to grips with technique 185
- Macro mode 185
- Supplementary lenses 186
- Extension tubes 187
- Reversed 50 mm 187
- Exposure 189
- Depth-of-field 190
- Using a flash 191
- Colour balance 191
- Scanning insects 191
- Tripods 193
  - Selecting a tripod 193
- Monopods 195
- Some final words of advice 195

Insect orders 197
Insect names English/Afrikaans 197
Pronunciation of insect families 199
References 200
Index 201

The "ears" of this katydid can clearly be distinguished just below the front knee joints while the mouthparts are those of a chewing insect.

Introduction

One winter morning a number of years ago, I was weeding a patch of Namaqualand daisies growing in my garden. I noticed a flash of colour as the sun reflected off a bright green object on the ground. I bent and picked it up – it was a small dead beetle about 25 mm in length. Drawn by its beauty I decided to take some photographs of it.

After going through the steps of setting up my camera and taking various photos of the beetle, now stuck to a lump of clay, I eventually had an image on my computer screen. It was only at this point, with the image enlarged on the screen, that I could clearly see what this little insect really looked like, and I was again struck by its remarkable beauty.

It had a small, somewhat pointed head with rather large eyes for the size of the head. I could see that it had well developed, protruding mouthparts which I assumed could only be used for chewing. There were also two prominent feelers just forward of the eyes, ending in flat pads that consisted of multiple parts. The thoracic area to the rear of the head was light brown. It changed to a darker brown around the edges and a very dark brown, almost black, at the rear edge where it seemed to form a collar. The whole thoracic area was smooth and shiny but the surface was dotted with numerous little pits which formed no particular pattern.

The most striking part of this creature, however, was its exquisite, gleaming green wing cases which subtly changed from green through to various shades of green-blue to violet depending on how the light caught them. Its iridescent hue and brilliant colour was indeed comparable in magnificence with the finest of semi-precious stones. Its wing cases were also pitted but in well-spaced, parallel lines, of which there were about eight on each side, running from front to back. The beetle also had three pairs of legs each with joints that could bend, knee-like, and that ended in tiny claws.

Little did I know that this small creature which so fascinated me and which I later learned was called an Amethyst Fruit Chafer with the imposing scientific name of *Leucocelis amethystina*, would lead me down a path that would keep me occupied with my camera for many years to come. It opened up a world of wonder and fascination that would eventually lead to the publication of this book.

This book is by no means intended to be a comprehensive dissertation on insects. To do that would be far beyond my capabilities as a dedicated but still aspiring amateur entomologist. What I intend to show you are those insects which have found their way in front of my camera's lens. After all, this book is primarily about the stunning beauty of insects.

By far the great majority of insects that I photograph are alive and doing what comes naturally to them in their environment. To this end I have spent many pleasurable hours looking in and under bushes, scratching around in the undergrowth and digging in the ground. However, from time to time, I find an already dead specimen or someone brings me an insect, alive or dead, worthy of being photographed. In cases such as these I set them up in my lab-studio to take photographs.

The identification of insects is, even under ideal circumstances, an extremely difficult and complex task with experts often disagreeing on the exact identification of certain specimens. Furthermore, many millions of species have never been identified or documented, while others require careful study, in some cases even dissection under a microscope, to differentiate one species from the next. The difficulty of identification is greatly compounded when specimens have to be identified from a photograph that often shows only one view and can sometimes only be scrutinised on the computer screen days after the insect has been photographed.

I have tried throughout to be as precise as possible in identifying my insect photographs by using in many cases opinions of experts and in others by consulting the best entomological reference material that I have been able to obtain. If, by chance, I have misidentified any specimens or allocated incorrect scientific names, I apologise. Any corrections or suggestions from knowledgeable experts will be greatly appreciated and can be included in future editions.

As to the general use of common names for insects it must be pointed out that these can be notoriously inaccurate as common names often change from region to region or different common names are used for the same insect even within a region. In spite of this, many people do more easily identify with the familiar common names used from day to day. For this reason I have used them throughout with the scientific names, where available, added in brackets. For the common names I have adopted the names given by Mike Picker, Charles Griffiths and Alan Weaving in their excellent publication, *Field Guide to Insects of South Africa*, published by Struik Publishers. I have also used this publication extensively to help me in the identification of many of my insect photographs.

With this, I would like to invite you to join me in the succeeding pages on a small safari through the wonderful, fascinating and beautiful world of insects.

A "green looper" larva showing in front the six true legs and at the rear end three sets of false legs (prolegs) which are used for added grip.

What is an insect?

Many common terms such as "insect", "gogga" and "bug" are frequently used to describe virtually any living creature that creeps or crawls or that lives on or under leaves. In entomological terms, an insect is a specific member of a specific group of the Animal Kingdom. Although the terms "insect" or "bug" are often used indiscriminately and interchangeably, it is necessary to clarify exactly what an insect is and which "bugs" are, in fact, not insects at all but members of other groups, such as the Arachnids which represent all spiders, scorpions and ticks.

The whole subject of taxonomy, which is the classification and naming of organisms, is a confusing one to say the least, with names changing from time to time and new orders or suborders being added, changed or scrapped. To compound this problem experts often disagree on exactly where in this great quagmire of Latin names and terminology a particular insect belongs.

Fortunately, the insect does not care and, at least from the point of an insect photographer or the casual observer, we do not have to concern ourselves beyond a basic understanding of how to go about identifying our subjects. The finer points of insect classification can be left to the expert entomologist who may often need to cut up a specimen, even to examine its genitalia, to determine its exact species.

For general purposes of classification and identification the Animal Kingdom is divided into a number of different groups decreasing in size and specific characteristics as they proceed down the scale:

- Phylum
- Class
- Order
- Family
- Genus
- Species.

Insects, like us, firstly belong to the Animal Kingdom. Thereafter they belong to the Phylum Arthropoda, which is divided into a number of classes of which insects belong to the Class Insecta. From the class level we progress to the level of order and it is from this point onward that insect enthusiasts need to familiarise themselves to be able to identify their subjects.

Insects are essential for the pollination of plants. Although many different insects contribute to this task, the honey bee is probably the best known of all pollinators.

Insects are classified into orders based on various anatomical characteristics such as their wings or mouthparts. Some of the larger orders are:
- Coleoptera – beetles
- Diptera – flies
- Lepidoptera – butterflies and moths
- Orthoptera – grasshoppers and crickets.

The various orders are in turn broken down into families and sometimes subfamilies, then into genus and finally species. A particular insect is always referred to by its genus and species. It is worth noting that the genus and species are printed in italics while the genus is also capitalised.

The common Honey Bee is thus classified as follows:
- **Kingdom:** Animalia
- **Phylum:** Arthropoda
- **Class:** Insecta
- **Order:** Hymenoptera
- **Family:** Apidae
- **Genus and species:** *Apis mellifera*

Amateur naturalists wanting to get involved in the study of insects and related species are often put off by the technicalities of naming and identifying specimens, especially as this also encompasses learning the many rather intimidating Latin names. In fact, once one becomes caught up in the subject and understands the basics of insect nomenclature it is not quite as frightening as it first appears. The great advantage of using scientific names is that they are understood worldwide as they do not change from one language to another.

The basics of insect anatomy

To the casual eye different insects may appear to differ greatly in appearance and structure from one another. Compare, for example, a mosquito with a dung beetle. Is it feasible that they can in any way be related and belong to the same class?

In fact, despite all the obvious differences in general appearance, all insects have common anatomical characteristics that place them in the Class Insecta. Insects have a body made up of three distinct parts. They also have six jointed legs and usually two pairs of wings.

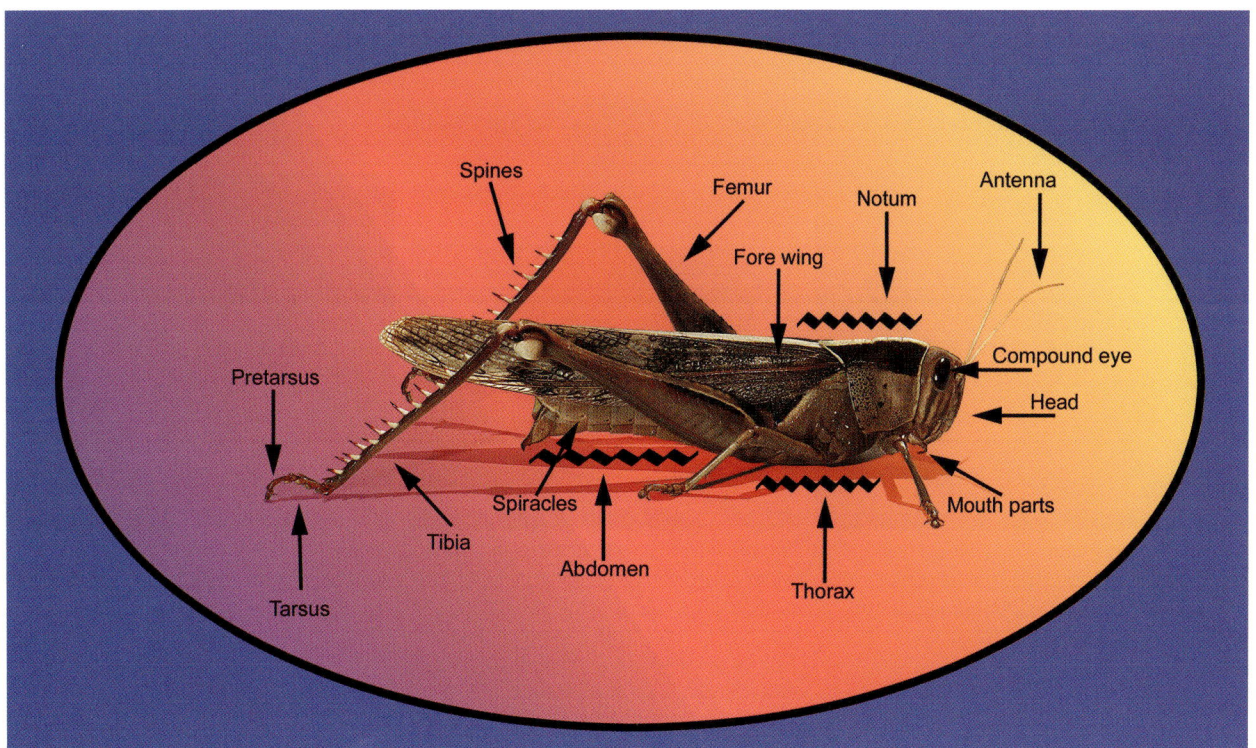

The parts of an insect's body

Fact File

- Insects are the most successful and diverse forms of life on earth.
- It is estimated there may be as many as 30 million different species of insects.
- Less than one million species of insects have been identified and named.

The three main parts of the body are the **head**, **thorax** and **abdomen**. Each part in turn consists of a number of segments.

The segments that form the head are fused together and difficult to tell apart. The mouthparts, a pair of antennae and the eyes are found on the head. There may be additional small eyes usually on the top of the head, called ocelli.

Mouthparts are specifically adapted according to the insect's diet and may be suited for chewing or sucking. Some have a short, strong, piercing **rostrum** for impaling prey while others have a long, delicate **proboscis** designed to reach and suck up nectar from deep inside flowers. Carnivorous insects often have well-developed, strong mouthparts used for both firmly holding as well as chewing their prey. Some insects such as assassin bugs can deliver a nasty bite if handled, as their sharp rostrums can easily pierce human skin.

Antennae, which function both as smell and as touch organs, differ greatly in length and structure. They are an important indicator used in the identification of insects and families in insect orders. The antennae can also pick up the very faint scent of highly complex chemicals called pheromones which many insects secrete to attract mates, sometimes over great distances.

The thorax consists of three segments, each of which carries a pair of jointed legs while the last two segments also each have a pair of wings.

The legs of an insect are jointed and consist of a **femur** or thigh, a **tibia** or shank and a **tarsus** or foot. The tarsus in turn also has several joints and usually ends in either a claw or pads. Many insects have legs that are specially adapted for catching or holding prey while the legs of others are used for digging, running, swimming and other activities necessary for their survival.

In many insects the wings are also adapted in various ways. For example, the forewings of many beetles are adapted into a hard protective shell called the **elytra**. In flies the hindwings have been adapted to form two small paddle-like organs called **halteres**. In other insects the wings may be almost non-existent except for small tubercles. The wings as well as the structure of the veins on the wings are important criteria by which different species are classified.

A close-up of the head of an assassin bug illustrates its sharp piercing beak or rostrum with which it sucks out its prey. Assassin bugs can deliver a nasty bite when handled. Body size ± 15 mm (*Phonoctonus* sp.).

The structure and form of the veins on the wings of an insect are important indicators used to determine species. Here the typical venation of the common house fly (*Musca domestica*) can be seen. What is characteristic is the way in which wing vein 4 bends upward to meet wing vein 3 at the margin of the wing.

A Carpenter bee (*Xylocopa caffra*) hovers close to a flower while patrolling its territory in a flowerbed. Carpenter bees are also valuable pollinators.

An insect's abdomen contains the breathing organs, heart, digestive system and sexual organs. Although there are no legs or wings on the abdomen, it does have a number of spiracles or breathing holes through which it draws air. The abdomen is a soft and sensitive part of the body. It is often protected by a hardened elytra and in many cases may even be difficult to see except from the underside of the body. Some insects such as certain ant species also have glands in the abdomen which release chemicals for self-defence.

The larvae of those insects that undergo a full metamorphosis may have no legs at all or they may have six true legs and up to ten additional **prolegs**. Prolegs are soft, unjointed appendages resembling legs that are used to grip the smooth surfaces of leaves and twigs. These false legs disappear when the larva pupates and reaches adulthood.

Insects do not have a skeleton in the conventional sense of the word. Instead of bones, they have an external skeleton or **exoskeleton** consisting of plates of a hard, durable material called chitin. As these plates cannot expand, the insect needs to shed its exoskeleton as it grows and replace it with a new and larger one which has formed beneath the existing one. This is called moulting.

Metamorphosis

Insects have unique ways of growing through different stages to reach mature sexual adulthood. They are not able to mate and reproduce until their final stage of development has been reached. With some insects this may entail a final moult and development of wings, while with others it may be the emergence from a pupa as a winged adult.

In the first case, immature insects called **nymphs** hatch from the egg looking very much like miniature versions of an adult. They then shed their skins a number of times as they grow larger until, in the final nymphal stage, wings develop. They are now adults and are referred to as **imagos**. This is called incomplete or **hemimetabolous** metamorphosis and is found in orders such as the true bugs (Hemiptera).

Complete or **holometabolous** metamorphosis, on the other hand, involves a life cycle where the egg hatches into a larva (maggot, grub or caterpillar). This larva then feeds, grows and moults a number of times before undergoing an inactive stage called a pupa, sometimes in a protective cocoon. The insect eventually emerges from the pupa as a winged adult. This form of metamorphosis takes place with, for example, butterflies and moths (Lepidoptera).

Fact File

Insects can be found everywhere.
Insects can be found in almost all terrestrial and freshwater habitats, from the driest deserts to freshwater ponds, from the canopy of a tropical rain forest to the arctic wastes.

A mantid nymph in the process of shedding its old skin against a background of coloured stones.

A newly emerged moth leaves its pupal case adhering to a twig.

THE ROLE OF INSECTS

It is by no means unusual to meet people whose general perception of insects is that they are either harmful pests that bite, sting or in other ways present various dangers or that they are revolting creepy-crawly creatures to be avoided or worse still, squashed without mercy. This unenlightened approach towards insect life, in fact towards all arthropods, is undoubtedly due largely to a lack of knowledge of the importance of these life forms and how they fit into the overall picture of life on earth.

Harvard biologist E.O. Wilson wrote, *"So important are insects and other land dwelling arthropods, that if all were to disappear, humanity probably could not last for more than a few months."*

This is an astonishing statement but one that places in dramatic context the vital role played by these creatures in the overall global ecosystem and ultimately in the well-being of our planet.

Insects have developed ingenious ways to protect themselves from predators, such as this mantis whose hindwings have been camouflaged so as to resemble a leaf.

FACT FILE

We need insects.

Insects are incalculably valuable to human beings. People usually think of insects in a negative context. Insects eat our food, feed on our blood and skin, contaminate our dwellings and transmit diseases. But we could not exist without insects. They are a fundamental part of our ecosystem.

Insects are in great part responsible for the breakdown of organic material such as plant, animal and human remains, the elimination of animal waste, the aeration of the soil and, of course, the vitally important task of plant pollination. They are an essential food source for many birds, fish, reptiles and amphibians, while in some parts of the world they also constitute a significant part of the human diet. Although the plight of endangered mammals is often given considerable exposure, insects and related species, many of which are endangered, receive little attention despite their importance.

More than a million species of insects have already been identified worldwide and it is conservatively estimated that at least an equal number but possibly many more still remain unidentified. From studies conducted by Terry Erwin of the Smithsonian Institute's Department of Entomology in Latin American forest canopies, the number of living species of insects has been estimated to be 30 million.

In spite of the fact that insects are one of the most abundant life forms on earth, with the number of insect species exceeding that of all other species combined, the use of insecticides, the proliferation of invasive alien vegetation and the encroachment into their natural habitats is having its consequence and insect populations are being alarmingly reduced or decimated.

Untold numbers of species have been adversely affected by people's selfish violation of rain forests, wetlands, bushveld and savannas. Many species, some possibly not even yet identified, are threatened or possibly already extinct while others are moving from their normal distribution ranges in order to survive.

Insect control in the past has often been highly irresponsible with the indiscriminate use of non-specific

The long, coiled proboscis of a butterfly allows it to reach deeply into a flower to extract nectar. Painted Lady butterfly (*Cynthia cardui*).

insecticides killing not only the pests but also all their natural predators and other valuable and harmless species. No doubt the present escalating global warming phenomenon will also have its effect on insect life. In many cases insects will either die or be displaced from their natural habitats due to the disappearance of their host or food plants. Another school of thought advocates that some species may increase greatly in numbers due to the stimulating effect of higher temperatures on their breeding patterns – this may, in turn, adversely affect other species.

This in no way implies that a "live and let live" policy should be adopted with relation to all insect life. Their very diversity, adaptability and ability to breed in vast numbers make judicious control of insect life essential to human well-being. Many insects are serious agricultural pests while others are instrumental in the spread of both human and animal diseases. The mosquito, tsetse fly, sandfly and others have wreaked havoc in many parts of Africa causing untold suffering and deaths.

The natural predators of insects such as other insects, reptiles and birds, are essential in maintaining the balance of nature and perform a vital role in controlling insect populations. Despite every effort, for example, people have never been able to control the common fly responsible for the transmission of many diseases. Without the help of spiders and the many other creatures that prey on them, for they are a high source of protein, disease-carrying flies have the potential to decimate humankind. One authority has estimated that if one were to remove all the insects that catch house flies, within one year the entire planet's surface would be covered one metre deep in the offspring of just one pair of house flies.

Fact File

Approximately:
- 5 000 dragonfly
- 2 000 praying mantis
- 20 000 grasshopper
- 170 000 butterfly and moth
- 120 000 fly
- 82 000 true bug
- 350 000 beetle
- 110 000 bee and ant species

have been described to date.

Responsible and enlightened authorities are becoming increasingly aware of the important role insects play in the overall ecological equilibrium as well as their value as indicators for conservation monitoring.

Entomologists and agriculturists are also increasingly using biological methods to control the numbers of crop-destroying insects by introducing natural predators of the unwelcome pest, its eggs, larvae or pupae, such as parasitic wasps and ladybird beetles.

In many countries positive steps are being taken to restore natural habitats and encourage the breeding of beneficial insects. In South Africa's Western Cape region, two damselfly species, the Cape Bluet and the Ceres Stream Damselfly, both thought to be extinct, were recently reported seen again after the removal of alien vegetation from their habitat.

Insects from the past

Insects have been around for a very, very long time. Many millions of years before even the first dinosaurs walked the earth, the insects had already established a firm foothold in the developing ecosystem of the young earth. In a co-evolving relationship with plants, insects were among the first animals to become terrestrial. Palaeobiological evidence suggests that this insect/plant relationship even then, as it still is today, was based on factors such as symbiosis and parasitism.

In some parts of the world fossil evidence of insect life has been found in rocks dating back to the Early Devonian age some 400 million years

1: A fossilised cockroach wing (*Samaroblatta parvula*). The cockroach is a highly successful insect and has changed little over the ages.

2: A fossilised dragonfly wing with an almost three-dimensional quality (*Triassoneura heidiae*).

3: An as yet unidentified fossilised beetle with the elytra spread wide.

4: The individual segments on this 200 million year old beetle's body can still be clearly seen.

ago. At first they crawled, walked and wriggled and then about 350 million years ago many species developed the ability to fly. By the Triassic period, some 100 million years later, insects were already well established and on the way to a tremendous expansion in species diversity.

In South Africa, the Molteno Formation in the semi-desert Karoo Basin had the richest known flora and insect fauna at about the time of origin of the mammals, dinosaurs and possibly the flowering plants in the Late Triassic period, about 225 million years ago.

At Birds River close to Dordrecht in the eastern Cape Province, a rich deposit of insect fossils, together with a large assortment of other fossilised material such as pteridophytes (ferns and their allies) and gymnosperms (cone-bearing, non-flowering seed plants) have been found of which some 350 insect species have already been identified.

Insect wings represent one of the primary ways in which many insects are classified and identified. Of special importance is the venation or pattern of veins of the wings which are distinctive for a specific species and act as "fingerprints" for identification. Fortunately, insect wings are also well suited to undergo the process of fossilisation and consequently serve to provide a valuable record of insect life in bygone ages.

Dragonflies (Odonata) are especially richly represented at the Birds River locality. In spite of the fact that dragonfly wings are thin and fine in structure, many have been preserved in exquisite detail in shale from what was a freshwater lake some 200 million years ago. In many of the fossils, wing bases as well as venation are clearly visible and study under a microscope reveals that even the finest detail has in several cases been preserved. In others the insect can be seen in its entirety, beautifully preserved in slate, shale or chert.

This opens up an extraordinary window into the early insect life in this part of the country. To the expert palaeoentomologist these fossils are a valuable source of research information. To laymen like ourselves, the fossils represent objects of fascination and rare beauty and are a reminder of the rich and long heritage of insect life on earth.

This fossilised wing of a mayfly that lived in the Karoo Basin some 225 million years ago has been beautifully preserved with its venation depicted in amazing detail.

A Robber Fly adopts a threatening stance seconds after having captured a small fly which it keeps firmly impaled on its proboscis.

FLIES
ORDER DIPTERA

The name Diptera means two winged and comes from the Greek "di" meaning two and "ptera" which means wings.

Flies make up one of the largest orders of insects both in their broad diversity of species as well as the number of individuals. Over 150 000 species have already been described worldwide while some 91 families are found in South Africa, with many demonstrating a great breadth of behavioural and ecological variation.

The Diptera have a long evolutionary history that extends back over 250 million years. They are unique as an order as they have only a single pair of wings compared with other insects which have two pairs. In all true flies the second pair of wings is present in the form of small club-shaped organs called halteres. These are found just behind the bases of the front wings and are attached to the body with sturdy but sometimes thread-like stalks. The length and thickness of these stalks as well as the size of the halteres in relation to the rest of the body vary greatly from species to species. On some species they

Many flies are dangerous carriers of pathogens as they breed in and feed on decaying matter.

Although they have only two wings, flies are superb aerialists. They can hover, fly backwards, turn in place and even fly upside down to land on a ceiling. They also have the highest wing-beat speed of any insect.

Flies fold their legs under the body when in flight then extend them, like an aircraft's landing gear, when they are about to settle. The arista (bristle) in the antennae of higher order flies is an air speed indicator. It allows the insect to sense how fast it is moving.

can clearly be seen with the naked eye while on others it is impossible to see them without magnification.

The fly uses its halteres for maintaining balance and stabilising flight. In effect they operate very much like miniature gyroscopes and are in a constant state of oscillation as the insect flies. This innovative adaptation of the basic insect wing has placed flies among the best aerialists in the world. They can fly forwards, backwards, upside down, hover motionless or make split-second changes in direction. Anyone who has ever tried to swat a fly or mosquito in flight will have experienced the almost uncanny ability with which members of the Diptera Order can take evasive action.

High-speed photography has shown that a house fly flying in a normal horizontal position is able to make an abrupt change of direction to the vertical, attach its forelimbs to a surface by means of the sticky pads on its feet and then flip itself upside down to come to rest, all in what appears to be one fluid motion. Although most flies are renowned for their speed and dexterity of flight, some members of the order are slow moving and avoid unnecessary flight. These include members of the Platystomatidae Family, some of which appear to be almost sluggish, as well as Crane Flies who are weak fliers and prefer hanging motionless, clinging to plants.

The Diptera have a tremendous ability to breed and it is this very ability for reproduction that make flies such an important link in the food chain by providing protein for many other species. The Diptera undergo a full metamorphosis, that is, from egg to larva to pupa and then to adult fly. During each of these stages they are preyed upon or parasitised. Adult flies and fly larvae and pupae are eaten by other insects, spiders, reptiles and amphibians, as well as by birds and small mammals. The larvae of many flies such as the Drone Fly and Mosquito, develop in water and consequently offer a nutritious meal to freshwater fish and other aquatic predators such as dragonfly larvae.

Flies are of great economic importance. Some are essential ecologically as pollinators and decomposers of dung, carcasses and other waste material while several species are predators and parasites of other insects. Many species, on the other hand, such as the Fruit Flies (Tephritidae), inflict crop damage while others are carriers of diseases and have a huge impact on the health of both animals and humans. The malaria-carrying Mosquito is said to be one of the greatest killers of humans. The Tsetse Fly, Black Fly, Flesh Fly and Blow Fly among others also spread deadly and disabling diseases.

Some flies such as the house fly have sponge-like sucking mouthparts.

Stable Flies, Mosquitoes and other "biting" flies have piercing mouthparts.

The Window-waisted Fly (*Hermetia illucens*) is a convincing wasp mimic. It has a strange anatomical feature in that it has a transparent "window" area between the thorax and abdomen.

The Platystomatidae family are a small family of large, slow-moving flies that are attracted to decomposing material such as rotten fruit, dead snails and even human faeces.

The Rock Fly (Family Lauxaniidae) is a slow-moving fly with patterned wings.

Some platystomatid flies such as this *Bromophila caffera* have prominent heads and a large proboscis; many also have patterned wings. Body length 30 mm.

A long-legged Crane Fly (*Nephrotoma* sp.).

FACT FILE

The little Scuttle Fly (Phoridae) is truly an omnivore. It has been experimentally reared on decaying vegetation, shoe polish, paint emulsions, human cadavers pickled in formalin and even lung tissue from living people.

Source: Department of Entomology, NC State University

A wasp-mimicking Syrphid Fly (genus *Ceriana*).

The Soldier Fly (*Ptecticus elongatus*) is another convincing wasp mimic. Body length ± 6 mm.

An Anthomyia Fly closely resembles a common house fly but is smaller.

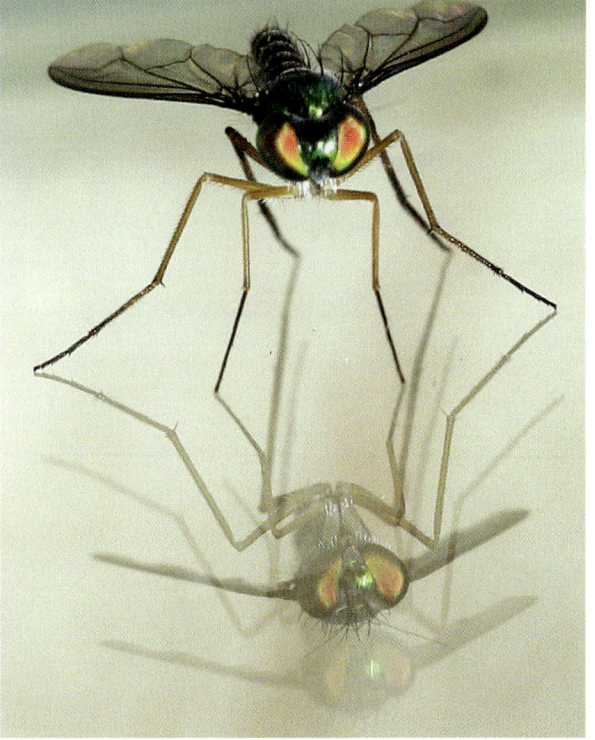
Long-legged Fly (Family Dolichopodidae possibly *Condylostylus* sp.).

Robber Flies
Family Asilidae

There are close to 4 000 species of Robber Flies throughout the world. Numerous species of Robber Flies are found in South Africa. Their interesting behaviour and somewhat striking appearance make them favourites among many Diptera enthusiasts, insect watchers and collectors.

Robber Flies are small to medium-sized insects ranging from 5–30 mm in length, depending on the species. They are common in gardens, especially in the vicinity of flowering plants where there is usually an abundance of other insects. They are fast-flying, relentless predators that prey on a variety of flying insects including other flies, bees and even wasps.

In general appearance the Robber Fly is usually black to grey in colour, with a notably hairy body. Most have long spiny legs further armed with bristles and powerful claws with which they capture and hold their prey. Some have a dense "beard" of bristles on the face. The head is large with two big compound eyes, each containing several thousand separate lenses. The Robber Fly is an opportunistic predator and has excellent binocular vision enabling it to spot even a small flying insect at a considerable distance and attack with deadly accuracy. It is armed with a robust dagger-like rostrum with which it pierces its prey. A fluid is then injected that kills the prey and liquidises it, enabling the Robber Fly to suck it dry.

The sharp spike-like proboscis of the Robber Fly (*Pegesimallus* sp.) is both a lethal weapon for impaling its prey as well as a mouthpart used for sucking out the body fluids of its victims.

The Robber Fly can usually be found in early summer sitting on a leaf, plant stem or sometimes a rock in an open sunny location, often close to a flower bed or flowering shrub. It continuously turns its head from side to side as it surveys the area for a potential victim. When a suitable subject is spotted, it will shoot off to seize the prey in flight and then settle down to enjoy its meal. This routine is repeated from time to time until the Robber Fly has satisfied its hunger.

It is interesting to note that the Robber Fly does not capture every insect it sees. Before attacking, it first briefly studies its intended victim from the air. If not to its liking, the Robber Fly leaves it alone and returns empty-handed. Many species repeatedly return to the same perching spot.

Robber Flies are fascinating subjects to study as they are not easily alarmed. If you move slowly and avoid any sudden movement, a Robber Fly can be approached closely before flying off. This is especially the case when it is busy eating. It remains engrossed in its meal allowing you to place a magnifying or camera lens within about 15 cm without becoming alarmed.

Compared to many other insects the mating behaviour of Robber Flies displays little or no courtship ritual. The male simply seizes the female much like he would a potential victim. They then interlock genitalia tail-to-tail. They usually perch on a twig in a shaded area but are also capable of limited flight during copulation.

Eggs are laid in various openings in bark, in the ground or on plants. After hatching, the larvae live in decaying organic matter or in the soil where they feed on other soft-bodied insects or on an assortment of other larvae. After pupating they emerge from the ground in adult form.

Fact File

Many flies are beneficial to humans. Some pollinate flowering plants, others assist in breaking down organic matter while some predacious flies serve as bio-control agents of other insect pests by preying on them.

Ever vigilant, a Robber Fly will inspect anything that moves but will attack only prey that it considers suitable. Many species are very specific as to which insects they eat.

While some Robber Flies are small, delicate insects others are squat and heavy and feed on bees, carpenter bees and even wasps.

Another hapless insect taken by a Robber Fly. It will inject its prey with saliva containing enzymes which will rapidly immobilise it and liquefy its tissues. All the body juices will be sucked from the prey and the empty shell discarded.

A pair of Robber Flies mate on a twig in the shade of a shrub.

Hover Flies
Family Syrphidae

One or other of the many species of Hover Flies, also known as Flower Flies, are sure to be found in almost every garden and can easily be recognised by their characteristic flight pattern. They typically hover almost motionless in the air, then suddenly zoom off a small distance in a forwards or sideways direction before hovering once again. This behaviour is repeated until a suitable plant or flower is found on which to settle and briefly feed. Then the whole cycle is repeated.

The Hover Fly with its striking yellow and black patterned abdomen and very large eyes is an exquisite little insect when seen from close up. The eyes of some species of male Hover Flies are so large that they cover almost the entire top and sides of the head, leaving place

Most of the head of a Hover Fly is dominated by its eyes. The eyes of the male are larger than those of the female and meet at the top of the head.

26 • Remarkable Insects

Hover Flies tirelessly patrol their area to keep intruding males out of their territory. They will often be seen hovering momentarily before suddenly shooting off in another direction.

only for a small pair of antennae. In size the Hover Fly may vary from 5–20 mm in length and many species are convincing bee or wasp mimics.

Although most adults feed on nectar and pollen, their larvae are avaricious eaters of aphids, mites, thrips and some caterpillars. Hover Flies are valuable insects to have in the garden not only because of their ability to control aphid populations but also because they are pollinators of significant importance.

They are typically found hovering about flower beds and appear to be especially attracted to members of the daisy family. During warm weather Hover Flies may at times occur in great numbers. The male can frequently be observed patrolling his mating territory and assertively chasing away any potential contender who may attempt to enter his domain.

This little Hover Fly (*Allograpta* sp.) – only about 10 mm long with a striking yellow and black abdomen and large red eyes – visits a daisy in search of nectar and pollen.

Some Hover Flies, such as the *Eristalis* species, lay their eggs in stagnant water. These aquatic larvae, which have an elongated breathing tube, are commonly called "rat-tailed maggots" while the adult is often referred to as a Drone Fly.

Hover Flies are important pollinators. In this finely detailed side view the many fine hairs on its body, to which pollen adheres, can be clearly seen.

A Hover Fly in full flight. Although they are known for their ability to hover helicopter-like they are also fast fliers and at times their wing beats can exceed 100 beats per second.

An Allograpta Hover Fly rests on a plant stem.

Hover Fly (possibly *Asarkina africana*) coming in for landing.

Another bee-mimic from the family Syrphidae to which all Hover Flies and Drone Flies belong.

Eristalinus taeniops, a very convincing honey bee-mimicking Hover Fly, is known for its black striped eyes. Also note the heavy proboscis as it prepares to suck nectar from a flower.

Hover Flies mate on a leaf. Note how the male strokes the head of the female with his forelegs.

BLOW FLIES
FAMILY CALLIPHORIDAE

Also known as Bluebottles or Greenbottles, Blow Flies are fairly large, robust, often metallic-coloured flies that frequent decaying plant and animal matter. The larvae of most species are scavengers and feed on carrion, excrement or garbage.

Blow Flies are usually the first insects to come into contact with a dead animal or human corpse and as such are important in forensic entomology. As their development through various stages of their life cycle is highly predictable if the ambient temperature is known, they can closely indicate the probable time of death of a deceased person.

Due to the nature of the matter they visit (dung, carrion), they are potential carriers of various diseases and can pose a considerable threat to human health if left to breed uncontrolled.

Recently significant international interest has been generated in "maggot therapy" where disinfected Blow Fly larvae (maggots) have been introduced into non-healing wounds of humans to clean out dead tissue in the wound and promote wound healing.

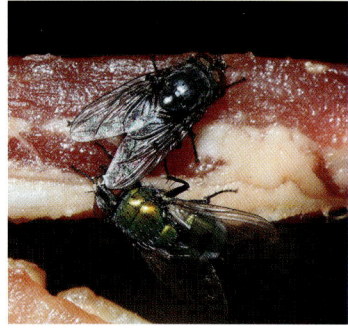 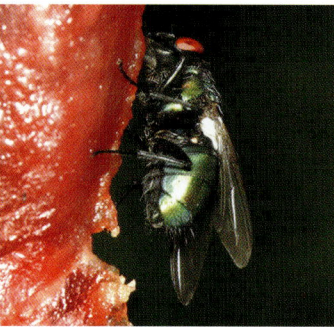 

Within minutes of hanging out a strip of rancid meat, Blow Flies begin to gather. They are also amongst the first insects to establish themselves on human or animal remains.

On settling, the Blow Fly will immediately begin looking for a suitable place on which to lay eggs.

A large number of eggs are quickly laid in a mass on the rotting meat, which offers the ideal conditions for their development.

Within 24 to 48 hours, depending on factors such as the ambient temperature, the eggs hatch into a wriggling mass of legless maggots.

After a few days, the maggots leave the meat and work their way into the ground where they pupate.

A day later, the pupae have darkened and within a few more days will emerge from the ground as Blow Flies, ready to repeat the cycle.

A close up view of the Regal Blow Fly (*Chrysomya marginalis*).

Fruit Flies
Family Tephritidae

Fruit Flies are serious pests with enormous economic consequences. In terms of agriculture they are possibly the most important family of flies with over 50 species found in South Africa. They attack a wide variety of fruits such as mangoes, avocados, apricots and guavas to mention just a few.

The female has a long, sharp ovipositor with which she pierces the skin of the fruit to lay her eggs in the flesh. After hatching, the larvae develop in the pulp of the fruit before tunnelling through to exit, leaving small exit holes.

Despite their potential for damage, Fruit Flies are handsome insects with beautifully patterned and shaded wings. Some have red eyes while others have eyes of iridescent green or blue. All are small in size with an average length of 3,5–5 mm.

The iridescent green eyes of a Fruit Fly (*Ceratitis* sp.).

A Fruit Fly shows off its intricately patterned wings.

A Mediterranean Fruit Fly (*Ceratitis capitata*). These little flies, measuring no more than a few millimetres, are responsible for devastating losses in the fruit industry.

Bee Flies
Family Bombyliidae

The Bombyliidae are a large family of flies with more than 900 species found in South Africa and at least 4 500 species worldwide. They are stout and hairy and, as their name implies, they are superficially rather bee-like in appearance. They are also about the same size, with some species being a little larger than the common honey bee.

Adults by and large feed on nectar and pollen. Many species have elongated mouthparts in the form of a long, tapering proboscis which they use for sucking nectar while hovering over flowers. While they are valuable pollinators of various plant species, their larvae are predators or parasitoids of eggs, larvae and pupae of a range of other insects such as beetles, wasps, solitary bees and grasshoppers.

Bee Flies can frequently be found in sunny locations hovering above blossoms in search of nectar and sometimes above bare patches of ground looking for suitable locations to lay their eggs, such as the open tunnels of solitary bees.

The larvae of the Bee Fly prey on the larvae and pupae of other insects such as solitary bees. The adult fly, however, feeds on nectar.

FLESH FLIES
FAMILY SARCOPHAGIDAE

Although Flesh Flies are often confused with the common house fly, they are larger and can easily be recognised from the combination of three strong black stripes on the thorax and a typically checkerboard patterned abdomen. They often also have bright red eyes.

Like Blow Flies, most Flesh Fly species breed in dung, carrion or decaying material. A few species place their larvae in the open wounds of mammals, hence their common name. They are also of great importance in forensic entomology to determine time of death. However, unlike the Blow Fly, they do not lay eggs on a corpse but deposit live larvae as the eggs hatch inside the female fly.

Flesh Flies can carry various diseases including leprosy bacilli and can also transmit intestinal diseases.

Flesh Fly (Family Sarcophagidae) showing characteristic checkerboard pattern on abdomen.

MOTH FLIES
FAMILY PSYCHODIDAE

Moth-like in appearance with broad, hairy wings and a hairy body, often with tufts of hair, these little flies are often mistaken for small moths by the casual observer but are, in fact, members of the Diptera Order. A close look reveals that like all flies, they have only two pairs of wings. A magnifying glass may be needed for this task as these insects really are tiny with a body length of about 4–5 mm and a total wingspan of less than 6 mm.

Moth Fly larvae are fungus eaters so Moth Flies are accordingly found near drains or soggy polluted areas where aquatic fungi thrive. They are also drawn to the smell of urine and are thus frequently encountered sitting on the walls of unhygienic toilets or bathrooms.

They perform a valuable service in the breakdown of fungi and bacteria at sewage plants where they normally breed in large numbers.

The adult Moth Fly (Family Psychodidae) is short-lived and does not eat. Its larvae, on the other hand, carry out an essential task related to the purification of sewage by the removal of fungus. Body length 4–5 mm.

Stalk-eyed Flies
Family Diopsidae

These strange looking flies have prominent eyes placed at the end of long stalks extending from either side of the head. Any specific advantage this unusual anatomical feature offers the insect in terms of hunting, feeding or survival is uncertain. Recent research by biologists of the University College London have indicated that female Stalk-eyed Flies typically prefer to roost and mate with males with the largest eye spans. The eye span of males also seems to play a part in the settling of territorial challenges between males and access to females.

Stalk-eyed Flies frequent warm areas and prefer a high humidity. They can often be found in shaded areas near streams where some species swarm in small groups. They are also prevalent in coastal regions.

Female Stalk-eyed Flies prefer males with the largest eye span.

Tachinid Flies
Family Tachinidae

Although Tachinid Flies are relatively diverse in appearance, most are bristly and about the same size as the common house fly. Many are yellowish in colour although some species may be drab or brightly coloured. Others are rather bee-like in general appearance.

Adult Tachinid Flies (*Gonia* sp.) feed on nectar. However, the larvae of all tachinids are parasites of other insects and feed on their internal organs.

The larvae of all Tachnid Flies are parasites of other insects which consequently makes the Tachinidae a significant family in natural pest control as many are noteworthy enemies of major pests. While some Tachinids attack caterpillars as well as adult and larval beetles, other species kill sawfly larvae, various types of true bugs, grasshoppers and other types of insects.

The female fly typically glues her eggs to the body of the host and conspicuous white eggs up to 1 mm in size can sometimes be seen on the head or body of a caterpillar or other host. After the eggs hatch, the maggots penetrate the host's body and proceed to eat it alive.

In some species, eggs are deposited on foliage near the host insect. After the eggs hatch, the maggots are ingested during feeding by the host, such as a caterpillar, and then develop inside the body of the host. Other species have a piercing ovipositor and actually insert the eggs inside the host's body.

Thick bristles characterise the Tachinid Fly (*Dejeania* sp.). This species has a red-flecked, balloon-like body.

Mosquitoes
Family Culicidae

The infamous Mosquito is a fly of immense medical importance and has even been called the greatest killer in the animal kingdom. Its life cycle, biology and behaviour have been studied in great detail in efforts to eradicate it but it remains a real menace in many parts of the world. Although in itself the Mosquito is harmless, certain species are carriers of numerous viral diseases and life-threatening organisms.

Only female Mosquitoes bite as they need the protein obtainable from a blood meal for their eggs to develop. Males feed on nectar or fruit juices. The mouthparts of a female Mosquito form a long, sheathed proboscis for piercing the skin of mammals to suck their blood. Some also feed on birds or even reptiles. Potential victims are located mainly through scent. Mosquitoes are responsive to the carbon dioxide

A female *Culex* Mosquito on a leaf in a pond of dirty water. Most species of Mosquito are very tolerant to pollution and will breed in even the foulest water.

in exhaled breath as well as several substances found in sweat.

Female Mosquitoes lay their eggs in water, either singly or in floating rafts of up to 400 eggs. After hatching, the Mosquito larvae also develop in the water feeding on micro-organisms. Pupation takes place in the water with the pupae rising to float just below the surface, to leave only once the adult stage has been reached.

Various insect predators such as robber flies and dragonflies help to control Mosquito populations while Mosquito larvae are fed upon by fish, tadpoles, dragonfly larvae and frogs.

Fact File

- Adult flies live in a wide range of habitats and display enormous variation in appearance and life style.
- There are more than 150 000 species worldwide.
- The Diptera probably have a greater economic impact on humans than any other group of insects. Some flies are pests of agricultural plants, while others transmit diseases to humans and domestic animals.

Male Mosquitoes (*Culex* sp.) have a handsome pair of feathery antennae and are larger than females. They do not suck blood but feed on nectar.

A female mosquito in typical resting position as seen from below.

Mosquito larvae (*Culex* sp.) are aquatic and although they cannot swim they can move about by vigorously wriggling their body. When threatened they rapidly sink to the bottom but soon rise to the surface again for air. The larvae breathe through a respiratory horn which is held just above the water.

Fact File

- Flies have the highest wing-beat frequency of any animal. In some tiny midges, it may be as high as 1 000 beats per second.
- Male mosquitoes are attracted by the wing-beat frequency, the characteristic mosquito "zoooom", of a virgin female.

When viewed close-up even a Stink Bug displays a kaleidoscope of colour.

True Bugs
Order Hemiptera

Hemiptera means "half wing" and refers to the fact that the first pair of wings is leathery, hard at the base and membranous at the tips.

The word "bug" is often incorrectly used as a collective term to refer to almost anything that creeps, crawls or has more than four legs. The bugs are, in fact, a distinct group of insects that can be identified by specific characteristics unique to Order Hemiptera. They are extremely diverse both in appearance and behaviour with species that have terrestrial, aquatic, semi-aquatic, tree-dwelling, burrowing and parasitic ways of life. In size they range from 1–110 mm in length.

As Order Hemiptera is so large and diverse, it is in turn split up into suborders, subfamilies and even superfamilies. Fortunately, we have no need to go into detail except to say that there are two main divisions. The Homoptera suborder includes those species that have uniformly textured wings such as the Aphids, Leafhoppers and other plant-sucking bugs while the Heteroptera includes all the rest.

Many of the plant-feeding bugs are of significant economic importance as they are serious pests of several crop plants. They may cause localised injury to plant tissues or weaken plants by removing sap while some also transmit plant pathogens.

The Heteroptera is a large suborder with a great diversity of species which are also known as true bugs. It is estimated that there are more than 50 000 species worldwide. Most have wings while some do not. Most are herbivorous but some are carnivorous and suck body fluids of other arthropods or even the blood of vertebrates. Many have glands that release foul-smelling substances. One thing that they all have in common is that they all have piercing-sucking mouthparts encased in a labium (lip) or rostrum (beak or proboscis). They are thus unable to chew material but feed only on plant sap or body juices which they obtain by piercing the food material. When not in use this proboscis is folded back under the body between the legs. Many species have a special groove under the body into which the proboscis fits.

Bugs do not undergo a full metamorphosis but develop by incomplete or hemimetabolous metamorphosis and thus have no larva or pupa stage. When young bugs hatch from the eggs they are structurally much the same as an adult except that they do not have wings. Dissimilarity in size, colour and camouflage can make them appear quite different to the casual eye.

The young bugs called nymphs then undergo a series of stages in which they shed their outer skin as they outgrow it. This usually takes place from 6 to 8 times depending on the species. During the final stages of growth wings are developed. Accordingly, all bugs which have wings have already reached the adult stage. Some species such as the common bed bug (Family Cimicidae) never develop wings.

The biology of the reproduction of some bugs, mainly members of suborder Homoptera, is unusual and complex. Some cicadas, for example, spend as long as 17 years underground as nymphs, feeding on roots, before emerging as adults. Some species of plant lice or aphids hatch first as wingless females that are capable of reproducing without males. This is called parthogenesis. After a number of generations winged females are then produced that migrate to different host plants. Only after still more generations and migrations are males and females produced that have the ability to reproduce sexually.

This Red-spotted Spittle Bug clearly shows the difference between the leather-like forewings and the membranous hindwings sticking out at the rear of the insect.

Although there are bugs that are carnivorous, most bugs live and feed on plants, seeds, fruits or pollen. Many are consequently serious agricultural pests. While some damage crops and ornamentals through their feeding several also have the potential to spread plant diseases.

This Assassin Bug is carnivorous and feeds on other insects. Bugs like these help to control the insect population.

Shield Bugs
Family Pentatomidae

Members of the Pentatomidae family of which there are more than 4 000 documented species worldwide and about 300 in South Africa, are frequently referred to as Shield Bugs or Stink Bugs. The name Shield Bug is derived from the sizeable triangular area called the scutellum between and sometimes also partially covering the wings which resembles the shape of a shield. In some species this shield is more noticeable and distinctive than in others.

The alternate name of Stink Bug refers to these insects' ability to discharge a bad smelling odour when threatened that serves to protect them from predators. In spite of their obnoxious smell Shield Bugs are often beautifully sculptured and colourful insects.

Most are crop pests as they feed on young shoots and buds while some species are also responsible for fruit malformation. A few species feed on insect larvae and caterpillars.

Fact File

- The Pentatomidae is a large family of bugs called Shield Bugs due to their shield-like shape.
- They can give off a foul smell, hence they are often also called Stink Bugs.
- The unpleasant smell is given off by a fluid which is produced by special glands on the underside of the abdomen.

A Shield Bug displays its bulbous compound eyes. A pair of simple eyes (ocelli) can also be seen on top of the head. This specimen has lost an antenna, quite possibly due to a confrontation with some predator.

1: The Bark Shield Bug (*Coenomorpha* sp.) is more commonly called a Bark Stink Bug.

2: Another member of the family Pentatomidae, dull coloured on top but bright red with black on the underside. Shield Bugs are found with a great variety of colour patterns.

3: Although Shield Bugs may appear ominous from close up the worst they can do is create a stink. These insects are armed with stink glands and release a foul smell when threatened.

4: A Shield Bug nymph in the process of shedding its old skin.

5: A colourful Antestia Shield Bug (*Antestiopsis orbitalis*) with its yellow spotted and finely pitted "shield" clearly displayed.

6: Close-up of a Bark Stink Bug (*Coenomorpha* sp.).

TRUE BUGS • 41

A brightly coloured Shield Bug with banded orange legs.

Nymph of Green Vegetable Bug (*Nezara viridula*).

Brown Shield Bug (*Dalsira costalis*). The black spot on each side of the thorax is diagnostic of this species.

Shield Bug nymphs.

Sunflower Seed Bug (*Agonoscelis versicolor*).

Newly hatched Shield Bug nymphs cluster around their egg cases.

SHIELD-BACKED BUGS
FAMILY SCUTELLERIDAE

The Shield-backed Bugs are also sometimes referred to as Jewel Bugs owing to the vivid gem-like colours of some species. They are generally a small group and in South Africa we find only about 30 species.

Shield-backed Bugs are often confused with beetles as they have a beetle-like appearance. They can also easily be confused with the Shield Bugs from the family Pentatomidae. A closer look reveals the differences. Firstly, Shield-backed Bugs have no split or line along the back as do beetles whose elytra consist of two parts. Secondly, their backs or scutella as a whole form a shield shape, whereas in the Shield Bugs only a triangular area on the back is shield shaped.

A Shield-backed Bug (*Solenostethium lilligerum*). The shield-like extension of the thorax is known as a scutellum and it covers the entire back of the insect giving it a beetle-like appearance.

Rainbow Shield Bug (*Calidea dregii*). The magnificent colouration of this bug illustrates why these insects are sometimes called Jewel Beetles.

ASSASSIN BUGS
FAMILY REDUVIIDAE

Assassin Bugs are fierce predators that feed on other insects and arthropods, some many times their own size. Sometimes they wait in ambush while at other times they actively stalk their prey and then use their powerful forelegs to capture and restrain it. They pierce the prey with the sharp stylets in the strong, curved rostrum and then inject both a toxin which paralyses the victim and digestive enzymes which liquefy the tissues. They suck up the body fluids, leaving only the hollow shell.

Assassin Bugs can be considered beneficial insects as they feed on other insects and thus help to reduce populations of many pest species. In some tropical areas such as South America species of Assassin Bugs belonging to the subfamily Triatominae are found which attack reptiles, birds and even humans, suck their blood and spread disease-causing organisms.

Assassin Bugs can inflict an extremely painful bite and will not hesitate to do so if handled. As their rostrum can easily pierce the human skin the possibility of secondary infections occurring is always present.

The Cotton-Stainer Assassin Bug (*Phonoctonus* sp.) mimics true Cotton-stainer Bugs, which then also form the Assassin's food source. Body size ± 15 mm.

FACT FILE

- Assassin Bugs feed by external digestion and can immobilise prey many times their own size.
- They probably also have the most painful bites caused by insects.

Metallic Assassin Bug (*Glymmatophora* sp.). With its mighty forelegs and strong piercing rostrum this assassin bug can deal with prey much larger than itself. It can also inflict a severe bite if handled.

An assassin bug (possibly *Acanthaspis* sp.) waits patiently for a potential meal. Assassin bugs are sometimes also called Ambush Bugs as they often wait in ambush for their prey to approach before pouncing.

Fact File

- Assassin Bugs are carnivorous and use their powerful forelegs to grab their prey.
- A toxic liquid is injected into their victim's body with the rostrum. This affects the nerves and liquefies the muscles and tissues of the prey. Once the insides of the prey are turned into a liquid, the Assassin Bug uses its rostrum to suck out the liquefied tissues.

Aphids
Family Aphididae

The tiny Aphid, most measure between 1–5 mm, are notorious for their ability to reproduce, making them one of the most pestiferous groups of insects worldwide. The life cycle of these insects includes both asexual or parthenogenetic and sexual reproduction. This life cycle may also include the production of eggs or live young depending on the cycle while adults can include winged or wingless forms.

Aphids are plant feeders and suck out plant fluids. If the Aphid population is large it will result in a significant reduction of the plant's vigour which may in time kill it.

Ants are invariably found with Aphids. Ants are their allies and protectors who often bring the Aphids to the plant. Ants eagerly "farm" and "milk" Aphids to collect a sweet honeydew excreted by the Aphids. This liquid can in turn serve as a medium for saprophytic fungi. These fungi grow on the leaf surface and reduce the photosynthetic properties and overall vigour of the plant.

Top left: Aphids cluster together on a plant. Their ability to reproduce in great numbers makes them highly destructive insects.

Above: A badly infested rosebud. The white cast-off skins of aphid nymphs can also be seen.

Left: Aphids are tended by ants who "milk" them for honeydew and also protect them. A drop of honeydew can be seen in the mandibles of the ant at the back.

Australian Bug
Family Margodidae

The Australian Bug (*Icerya purchasi*) also known as Cottony Cushion Scale is a native of Australia which has spread to many parts of the world. It has become a pest infesting many cultivated plants and presents a threat especially to citrus crops. Although nymphs are mobile the adult bugs are not. They attach themselves to the stems of plants, suck out the sap and retard the plants' growth or even kill it.

The Australian Bug has a reddish brown body to which is attached a white fluted egg sac containing up to 1 000 eggs and nymphs. Although winged males are at times produced, the bug is a hermaphrodite, meaning that it is both male and female and can thus fertilise itself. The red nymphs are tiny, about 1–2 mm in length. As they grow, they leave the egg sac and move about the host plant until a suitably soft stem is found in which they can insert their rostrums. Here they remain, mature and produce their own waxy egg sacs which they then proceed to fill with eggs.

Above: Within the egg sac of the Australian Bug there are hundreds of eggs and nymphs that will remain there until they mature.

Right: The Australian Bug. The brownish portion on top is the bug itself, which is attached to the plant by its proboscis. The white cottony portion below is the egg sac.

Twig Wilter Bugs
Family Coreidae

Twig Wilter Bugs are also commonly known as Leaf-Footed Bugs as the males of some of the species found in this family have enlarged femora or hind legs with projections resembling the shape of a leaf. These projections may also carry hardened, inward-pointing spines which are presumably used for territorial defence.

Twig Wilters are large conspicuous bugs with some reaching a size of up to 40 mm. They feed on the stems and young shoots of plants, sucking out the plant juices and causing serious wilting of the plant in areas where they have fed.

Some species of Twig Wilters have the ability to discharge a defensive fluid which they can squirt for a considerable distance when threatened. They can also give off a foul-smelling liquid from scent glands located between the bases of the middle and hind legs.

A Twig Wilter Bug. These bugs feed on shoots, withdrawing the plant sap and causing the shoots or twigs to wilt. Most have prominent veins in the membranous part of the wings; some species also have enlarged hind legs (femora).

Left: A Twig Wilter Bug (possibly *Homoeoceris* sp.) with proboscis folded under the body seeks a suitable spot to feed.

Above: A closer look at a large Twig Wilter Bug (*Carlisis wahlbergi*). Note the enlarged femora of the hind leg. Twig Wilter Bugs are also capable of giving off a foul smelling liquid which is discharged from openings at the base of the hind legs. Body length 25 mm.

Treehoppers
Family Membracidae

If ever you sit in your garden in the shade of a tree, and see what appears to be a thorn moving about on one of the branches or on a nearby shrub, do not be alarmed. You are not hallucinating – you have probably just spotted a Treehopper.

These weird little insects have a body length of no more than 4–6 mm. The upper part of their thorax or pronotum extends into strange thorn-like structures. Unless they move they are virtually impossible to detect and appear to be no more than a natural protrusion on a branch.

They feed on the sap of woody plants and although there are over 100 species found in South Africa, they are shy and rarely noticed by the casual observer. The name Treehopper appears to be somewhat of a misnomer as I have yet to see one hop. When disturbed, they slowly move away, often just to the other side of the branch on which they are sitting. Sometimes they may fly away. They are not found only on trees but also frequent other plants and shrubs.

Main picture: Treehopper. This unusual little creature with a body length of only about 5 mm mimics a thorn as it sucks sap from a plant stem.

Inset: Another species of Treehopper (*Oxyrachis* sp.) also with thorn-like projections. Note the beautifully veined wings.

A family of Treehoppers, two adults and a nymph.

Treehoppers are nurtured and protected by ants that obtain a sweet substance called honeydew from the bugs. Here an ant "strokes" a Treehopper to encourage it to produce honeydew.

Fact File

- The Treehopper feeds on the sap of woody plants.
- This strange little insect mimics a thorn to avoid predators.

Some species are tended by ants who appear to stroke them to obtain honeydew that they secrete. They are quite satisfied to remain quietly feeding while little black ants scuttle all over them.

Leafhoppers
Family Cicadellidae

Leafhoppers are tiny, delicate insects, about 2–3 mm in length. They have large eyes on the side of the head and finely veined wings. Although they are usually green or blue-green in colour, there are also species which are predominantly blue or red. Many have almost triangular, rounded or broadly curved heads. Their

It is surprising to find such a delicate insect as the Leafhopper armed with such a heavy set of spines on the hind leg.

The little Leafhopper usually feeds on the underside of leaves and is capable of transmitting many plant diseases. They are strong jumpers and can also fly, allowing them to easily move from plant to plant.

hind legs have either one or two rows of prominent spines.

Leafhoppers belong to a family with a large diversity of species. There are at least 20 000 species already documented and new species are discovered on a regular basis. Due to their size and colouration, they are generally inconspicuous and not readily seen by the casual observer. If disturbed, they quickly hop away.

It is common to find Leafhoppers in grassland but they also feed on many different types of plants. As they are exceedingly prolific and produce several generations a year, they present a real threat to cultivated crops as well as to the gardener. They normally feed on the underside of leaves and, like all bugs, have a piercing proboscis which they use to extract plant sap. Although their presence can cause whitening and curling of the leaves on which they feed, their real danger is as vectors of pathogenic viruses and other plant diseases.

Fact File
- Leafhoppers are one of the most common and abundant groups of herbivorous insects.
- It is estimated that the actual number of Leafhopper species may exceed 100 000.
- Leafhoppers are an important food source for predators such as birds and lizards as well as spiders, assassin bugs, wasps and robber flies.

Spittle Bugs
Family Cercopidae

The presence of Spittle Bugs is more often than not first detected when a shrub or tree is seen to be dripping

A Red-spotted Spittle Bug (*Locris arithmetica*) feeding on a grass stem.

considerable quantities of sticky fluid which appears to originate from its branches. Closer examination of the plant reveals that this liquid comes from a large ball of what appears to be white froth. This is the home of the Spittle Bug nymph and is produced by mixing extruded plant sap with air and a waxy substance, thus causing it to foam. Copious quantities of sap are taken from the plant and pass through the insect's body with only a small amount retained for nutrition. The rest is used to form the ball of cuckoo-spit, as it is sometimes called.

The Spittle Bug lives and moults in this foamy cocoon which serves to protect it from drying out in the sun as well as from attack by predators. The nymph is seldom seen unless the frothy ball is scraped away. Nymphs often nest close to each other which results in almost entire branches being covered in foam. At a certain stage the nymph leaves the nest, moults once more and then matures into the adult insect.

Adult Spittle Bugs can jump and fly. They feed on a variety of plants and grasses from which they suck the sap.

Twig Snout Bugs
Family Fulgoridae

Snout Bugs are often called Lantern Bugs stemming from an erroneous belief in the past that they emitted light when mating. Be that as it may, they remain curious looking creatures with the Twig Snout Bug being one of the more unusual species. A mottled grey colour, it has an extension to the head which gives it the appearance of a broken twig. Some species of Snout Bugs are also brightly coloured.

The natural camouflage of the Twig Snout Bugs makes them difficult to spot as they are only about 28-30 mm in size. They are, however, attracted to lights and this particular specimen was rescued from a spider web located just below an outdoor lamp.

The powerful spined forelegs of the mantid are formidable weapons from which few victims will ever escape once in their grasp. When ready to attack, the mantid holds these legs folded in front of the body. When a potential target approaches they are shot out and the prey is gripped scissor-like between the spines.

Mantids
Order Mantodea

The name derives from the Greek word for a prophet or seer.

Mantids, the veritable dragons of the insect world, have often been called "the strangest of all insects". Throughout the centuries they have been feared and revered by many cultures. Some believed them to be soothsayers, others the bringers of good luck. It has even been said that their saliva could poison cattle.

Certainly the mantids are unique in the insect world. Their exceptionally mobile heads that can turn from side to side, large compound eyes, super strong raptorial forelegs and split-second reflexes make them formidable killers. Some mantids look like dried leaves, twigs or flowers while others may be green, brown, speckled or adorned with leaf-like appendages on their legs or abdomens. As a group they are best known for the characteristic stance that they adopt while waiting for prey with forelimbs held upright in front of the head. This "prayer-like" position has also led to the names Praying Mantid or Praying Mantis being used.

Left: A cryptically patterned mantid waits expectantly on a branch for an unsuspecting victim to approach. Its camouflage makes it almost indistinguishable from the bark.

Centre: When a prospective meal is detected the mantid readies itself for attack by drawing up its forelegs. Apart from this quick movement it remains motionless.

Right: The hapless victim, a Twig Wilter Bug, moves within striking range and in an instant the mantid reacts. It has secured a tasty meal which is grasped firmly in the grip of its forelegs.

The Mantodea are a widespread order of insects with just under 2 000 species found worldwide of which about 120 species are encountered in southern Africa. Many mantids such as the Green Mantid as well as Leaf, Flower and Bark Mantids often frequent gardens where they can be found on shrubbery or tree trunks patiently awaiting the approach of suitable prey. Despite the large size of most mantids, they are easily overlooked as they are masters at camouflage and are capable of blending seamlessly into the background foliage. Some Green Mantids develop intricate leaf-like markings complete with holes and other defects, while Bark Mantids imitate the texture and colour of tree bark. Others may be mottled in appearance, with grey, white, black and tan colouration.

Mantids are attracted to light and often enter houses where they happily settle on a curtain rail or other convenient spot and patiently wait for their dinner in the form of insects which have found their way indoors after the light.

The mantid's powerful mandibles are capable of dealing with an assortment of prey. It will eat bugs, beetles, cockroaches, crickets, grasshoppers and whatever else it is able to capture. Mantids only eat live prey and will not accept anything that is dead.

Like other insects, mantids have six legs but the mantid uses only its last two pairs of legs for walking. The strong raptorial forelegs have been specially adapted for capturing and holding its prey which generally consists of moths, butterflies, flies and crickets, although it will take virtually all nature of insects, some even larger than itself. These legs are moved by large, strong muscles

The Praying Mantid, or "Praying Mantis" as they are often called, is able to turn its head from side and can look around for prey without having to move the rest of its body. It is the only insect able to do this. Moreover, with its well-developed compound eyes the mantid misses no movement (*Sphodromantis gastrica*).

and are also armed with a number of sharp, tooth-like, hardened spines. Any hapless insect caught in the grip of these spines has no chance of escape whatsoever.

Mantids do not actively hunt their prey but rather ambush them. A mantid sits entirely still, only occasionally moving its head to follow any movement in its proximity, until some unsuspecting creature approaches within its range. Then it rapidly shoots out the forelegs which are always held at the ready, and snaps up its dinner. It is not without reason that they are known as one of the insect world's deadliest predators.

Mantids eat their prey alive. I have often watched mantids catching insects and they invariably seem to turn their prey in their grasp and always start by eating the head first. Whether this is characteristic of all mantids I cannot say, but it certainly is the case with those that I have studied and I have seen a variety of different species do the same thing.

Mantids have voracious appetites and never seem to be put off from a good meal. Even when threatened, for example when being photographed and gently prodded to move into a required position, they will not release their prey. Certain species, however, will flare open their often brightly coloured hindwings in a threatening display when disturbed. Although they are tyrants in the insect world and have powerful jaws capable of dealing with any prey that they can capture, they are harmless to humans. Larger specimens, however, can deliver scratches with their sharp spines if handled carelessly.

Mantids have the ability to swing, turn and tilt their heads which most other insects do not have. This, together with their triangular-shaped head and large alert pair of prominent compound eyes which seem to stare directly at one, make them appear very much like small aliens from another planet.

Although most adult mantids have wings, they are rather clumsy fliers and do not often take to the air.

FACT FILE

- Mantids can turn their heads from side to side. They are the only insects able to do this without moving any other part of the body.
- They have simple eyes called ocelli as well as well-developed compound eyes which give them excellent vision.

Above left: Long and slim, a Grass Mantid (*Pyrgomantis rhodesica*) sits on a dried grass stalk.

Above right: A Cone-headed Mantid (*Idolomorpha dentifrons*) cleans its long hind leg. Body length 85 mm.

Left: An alien looking Cone-headed Mantid.

A strikingly patterned Bark Mantid sits in alert readiness.

A Gargoyle Mantid nymph (Family Empusidae) perched on a stem of wild grass.

A Cone-headed Mantid patiently awaits its prey. Body length 85 cm.

A bizarre little Leaf Mantid nymph (*Phyllocrania paradoxa*) with leaf-shaped legs and abdomen. This creature will become practically invisible against a background of dried leaves. Body length ± 12 mm.

Compare the size of this mantid's huge and powerful forelegs with the rest of its slim and rather frail looking body.

during the mating process. Although this behaviour does sometimes take place, it is apparently not as common as is generally believed. The reason for this strange behaviour is also uncertain with some authorities believing that it only happens when the male has not grasped the female in exactly the right position, causing the female to experience him as a threat rather than a mating partner. Others believe that the female requires the additional protein for the development of her eggs and sees the male as a good source. However, undaunted, the resolute male mantid can continue with copulation even after his head has been bitten off as the nerves controlling this action are situated in the rear part of the abdomen.

After mating the female lays clusters of eggs, usually on a twig or branch, which she then covers with a frothy liquid that later hardens to a hard protective shell called an ootheca.

They much prefer to remain sitting motionless than fly about. Their forewings are somewhat narrow and usually leathery while the hindwings are larger and fan-shaped. In some species such as the ground-dwelling varieties as well as some females, the wings may be reduced or even absent.

Female mantids have become infamous for their bizarre habit of occasionally devouring the much smaller males

I have on a number of occasions while photographing mantids, experienced them repeatedly trying to climb from the foliage where they have been sitting onto the camera lens. When doing close-up photographs the front of the lens is about 100–150 mm from the insect. I can only suspect that they are seeing their own reflection or more likely the reflection of their own movements in the lens and are attempting to follow this.

With a flash of colour a tiny wasp launches itself from a leaf. This is possibly a member of the Ichneumonidae family of wasps.

Ants, Bees and Wasps
Order Hymenoptera

The name Hymenoptera means "membrane wings" and is derived from the Greek words "hymen" meaning membrane and "ptera" meaning wings.

The Hymenoptera Order includes all the stinging insects and most of the social insects. They are a large and diverse group that consists of an estimated 300 000 species worldwide with more than 100 000 species documented and described. In total there are about 70 families of Hymenoptera found in South Africa, each family containing many different species.

The Hymenoptera Order is divided into two suborders, namely the Aprocrita which includes all the ants, bees and wasps and the smaller Symphyta in which the sawflies are accommodated.

Members of the Aprocrita suborder are found in abundance in nearly all terrestrial habitats throughout South Africa. Any flowering plants from the smallest Karoo succulent to giant flowering trees benefit from their presence for, as a group, they are unparalleled as pollinators.

The suborder Symphyta is not as abundantly represented in South Africa as in many other countries.

Although some species of ants, sawflies and gall wasps may generally be regarded as pests, the overwhelming majority of Hymenoptera species are enormously beneficial, either as natural enemies of other insects or as pollinators. Some are also valued for their ability to supply useful products for human use and consumption such as beeswax and honey. In fact, from an economic point of view, they are considered to be the most beneficial order of all insects.

Most adults of the Hymenoptera Order have two pairs of wings of which the hindwings are smaller than the forewings. Exceptions include worker ants and some species of female wasps which have no wings. In flight, the hind- and forewings are linked to each other by a series of tiny interlocking hooks called hamuli which run along the leading edge of the hindwings. These hamuli hook into a fold near the back of the front wings to create one smooth aerodynamic plane which gives the insect excellent flying ability and agility. Wasps of the Vespidae family also have the ability to fold their large forewings along their length while at rest.

Although some species are specialised in their diet, Hymenopterans in general feed on a wide range of foods from fungus, seeds and nectar to other insects. Their mouthparts are suitably adapted for either lapping, sucking or biting and chewing depending on the species. The bees, for example, have a soft, flexible tongue formed by the lower lip or labium which curls downwards and inwards to form a tube up which nectar can be sucked.

All Hymenopterans are active insects constantly moving about either hunting, feeding or zealously working on their nests or hives.

Fact File

- Ants, bees and wasps, members of the Hymenoptera Order, are the only insects except for termites which belong to the order Isoptera, to have developed sophisticated social systems in which labour both in and out of the nests is shared by other members.
- Ants, bees and wasps are the only insects that can sting.

Hymenoptera is the only order of insects that has members capable of stinging. In many species the female's egg-laying organ or ovipositor has been modified for piercing or stinging and, in the case of the sawflies, for sawing. It is thus only the female that can sting as the males have no stinging apparatus.

Bees have a number of tiny barbs on their stinging organ which gives it the quality of a fish hook. Once it has been inserted it cannot easily be extracted as the barbs keep it firmly in place. A bee is therefore only able to sting once as the stinger is torn from its body when it attempts to withdraw it and the bee subsequently dies. The stingers of wasps and ants, on the other hand, are smooth and they can insert and extract them with ease, allowing these insects to sting repeatedly.

When any of these insects sting they also simultaneously inject a toxin, the strength and type of which varies from species to species. Stings from some species are relatively mild while others can be extremely painful. Many can also trigger life-threatening allergic reactions in some sensitive individuals. What is said to be one of the most painful stings of all, comes from a hairy and wingless little

Numerous wasps are only a few millimetres long yet many perform a beneficial service by controlling the numbers of other insects through parasitising their pupae and larvae. Most of these tiny species are difficult to identify individually without careful microscopic examination.

A small Mason Wasp explores the leaves of a fragrant herb.

wasp called the velvet ant (Family Mutillidae), where the female looks very much like an overgrown ant.

Hymenopterans are with the exception of certain species, generally docile insects, quite happy to go about their tasks of gathering pollen or building nests. When away from their nests or hives they only resort to stinging if directly threatened, such as when they are picked up, stepped on or trapped. Some members of the Hymenoptera Order, however, are highly organised social insects that live in large communal nests or hives and will vigorously defend their nests using their stings.

Various factors seem to affect the mood and aggression of these insects, of which the prevailing temperature of the day is one which appears to have a strong influence. On a warm day bees may be seen clustering in the entrance and on the outside of their hives, frantically flapping their wings to introduce an air flow into the hive to cool it down. When this happens, they become highly irritated and may turn on an innocent passer-by without warning, attacking in their hundreds.

Some of the paper wasps of the family Vespidae are even more easily irritated and do not seem to need the added stimulus of high temperatures to cause them to act aggressively. Just approaching a wasp nest too closely at any time could be considered a threat and reason enough for an attack.

Except for termites which, by the way, are not related in any way to ants and belong to a completely different order called Isoptera, ants, bees and wasps are the only other insects to have evolved complex social systems with division and sharing of labour and functions within the system. Not all members of this order are social. While some species may share hives or nests with many thousands of other individuals, others prefer a solitary existence. Many bees do not live in beehives and many wasps do not live in wasp nests but construct their own individual nests in the ground, in dried wood, in trees or in plant stems. There are no ants that live alone as all are communal and share large nests.

The Hymenopterans have also developed sophisticated means of communication involving senses such as sight, smell, touch and possibly other factors which are not yet fully understood. The well-known, complex and elaborate dance performed by honey bees is one example. Through this dance bees communicate to the hive the presence of food as well as the direction and distance from the hive at which it can be found. The exchange of information between ants through the touching of their antennae when they greet each other on a food trail is an occurrence which has undoubtedly been witnessed by even the most casual of observers. I have also seen paper wasps (*Polistes* sp.) demonstrating similar behaviour when two or more settle on a leaf.

Chemical communication plays an important part in the life of the Hymenoptera and the chemical or pheromone signals given off by bees and wasps when they feel threatened can send a nest or hive into an aggressive frenzy. The group of wasps known as paper wasps, many of which often nest under eaves or overhangs are particularly aggressive by nature. Accidentally injuring one, for example by stepping on it, will cause it to release pheromones. If this should take place in close proximity to a nest it will result in an alarm signal being sent out and immediate reprisal by hundreds of the inhabitants of the nest can be expected.

Ants

Although there are many similarities between ants, bees and wasps, ants have evolved even more successful and flexible ways of living as a group. They have a vastly complex social system with highly developed social habits which include their ability to work together, for example to move heavy prey. Ants also interact with other insects such as aphids, scale insects and treehoppers which they protect, herd and exploit to obtain honeydew while they welcome certain beetles and larvae into their nests.

They are the most widespread of the Hymenoptera and can be found everywhere on earth except in areas permanently covered in ice or exceptionally dry desert conditions. There are at least 10 000, but probably many more, species of ants worldwide with at least 2 000 species encountered throughout Africa.

An ant obtaining honeydew from a scale insect.

A Myrmicinae Ant scrambles over an African Potato plant. Note the 2-segmented waist.

The antennae of an ant are highly developed organs which are responsible for both the senses of touch and smell. In one species of ant more than 200 olfactory cones have been counted.

An ant "strokes" an aphid to induce it to release honeydew.

An ant carries away a foe. Ants often raid the nests of other ants. Notice the dead ant is winged.

Ants will overcome seemingly insurmountable obstacles to drag prey to their nests.

The mandibles of the worker ant are robust tools which also double up as potent weapons.

They differ from bees and wasps as their colonies are permanent and not started afresh each year as those of the wasps and wild bees. Ants' nests can last for 10 to 30 years if left undisturbed and consist of anything from a few hundred ants to millions of individuals. Ants are also exceptionally long-lived. A queen ant can live up to 15 years and some workers live for 5 or 6 years.

As a group they are remarkably adaptable and able to survive under greatly varying conditions. Whereas bees and wasps construct their nests according to fixed patterns where the shape and size of their cells are consistent and specific materials are needed for their construction, ants do not stick to any fixed plan. They can change their habits according to existing conditions and make their nests of whatever material is available. This is one reason why ants survive so well.

Ants are tireless travellers and often cover long distances in search of food. They can climb vertical

Ants gather up their larvae and pupae.

surfaces such as tree trunks, plant stems or walls with ease and make their way through or around virtually any obstacles to reach a food source. They exist on a varied diet which includes other insects, plant juices,

African Thief Ant (*Carebara vidua*). The females of these ants have a body length of about 25 mm. Thief Ants prey on termites.

A winged male of the Red Driver Ant (*Dorylus helvolus*). These large ants can reach a length of up to 50 mm.

times their own weight back to their nests.

Scouting ants lay down a chemical trail when a food source has been discovered and soon this trail is followed by hordes of worker ants. Just pulling a finger across this trail at any point breaks the link and thoroughly confuses the ants who then run about until they have once again picked up the trail on the other side of the finger smear. If a deviation has been taken around the intrusion, a new trail is laid and the ants then follow this deviation.

Apart from their obvious nuisance value in homes and gardens ants do more good than bad. They play an essential part in aerating and turning the soil with their tunnelling and also help in the transportation of organic material into the ground. Possibly one of their greatest beneficial achievements, however, is the control of termite populations. Many ant species relentlessly raid termite nests eliminating millions of these destructive pests.

A number of carnivorous beetles feed on ants as do certain spiders. Some wasps collect ants for their larvae while other insects such as antlions and mantids prey on them. They also form an important part of the diet of many birds and reptiles. In spite of this and the best efforts of humans to exterminate them in certain areas, ants keep spreading and ant colonies keep growing. It has become an accepted fact that although ant colonies can at best be controlled, they can seldom be exterminated.

Both male and female ants develop wings and can be seen in great numbers in spring and summer, usually just after good rains, when they undertake their nuptial flights. After being fertilised, the females shed their wings before founding a new colony as queens or re-entering their parent colony. When the mating flight is over the males die.

seeds and fungus which they often cultivate and they will also accept a great variety of other substances such as household sugar and crumbs. This ability to adapt their diet to whatever is available is another strong factor in their successful survival as a group. They are also exceptionally strong insects and can carry objects many

BEES

Contrary to general perceptions, not all bees live in beehives and make honey. There are about 20 000 known species of bees worldwide and in all probability many more that have not yet been identified. About 90% of all bee species do not live in communally shared hives or colonies but build individual nests. The nests of these solitary bees may be found in the ground, in the stems of plants, in cracks or crevices in walls or in wood. Very often large numbers of nests may be found grouped together in close proximity. This, however, does not indicate social nesting but rather that conditions at that particular spot are suitable for the species concerned to build their nests.

One of the Cuckoo Bees. This solitary bee lays its eggs in the nests of other bees (*Thyreus* sp.).

Solitary bees do not have workers as honey bees do and neither do they have queens. All females are fertile and build their own nests in which they lay their eggs. The nests are usually stocked with nectar and pollen and then sealed off, leaving the brood to take care of themselves. Some of the solitary bees are parasites and lay their eggs in the nests of other solitary bees. These bees are commonly called cuckoo bees.

Although solitary bees visit flowers and gather both pollen and nectar in very much the same way as honey bees do, this is mainly to feed or to gather food for their brood. Although they do not make honey or beeswax and in this respect are of no commercial consequence, solitary bees are important as pollinators.

The tiny little *Allodapula variegata* is only about 8 mm. long. It is a solitary bee and lives in plant stems.

Carpenter Bees
Subfamily Xylocopinae

The name Carpenter Bee is derived from the manner in which these solitary bees hollow out tunnels in soft wood and timber in which they build their nests. The female Carpenter Bee excavates a round tunnel of about 1 cm or slightly larger in diameter and sometimes up to 20 cm long. Deep inside this tunnel she provisions a cell with a mixture of plant nectar and pollen, known as bee bread, on which she then lays a single egg before sealing it off. Another cell will then be started above the sealed cell and the process repeated until there are about six to eight cells in the tunnel each containing a quantity of bee bread and an egg. When the eggs hatch the bee larvae feed on the stored food. They then pupate in their individual cells, before finally making their way out as adult bees.

Carpenter Bees of the species *Xylocopa* are found throughout the country and can often be seen visiting flowers or hovering above flower beds. They are somewhat larger than honey bees and are often referred to as bumble bees. This is somewhat of a misnomer as bumble bees are not found in South Africa at all. The female Carpenter Bee is black with two white or yellow belts across the abdomen while the male is yellow and rather hairy in appearance.

The male Carpenter Bee may often be seen patrolling a small fixed area as it seeks to defend its territory from other males. Should a rival male be reckless enough to enter this area, it is angrily met head-on and a noisy confrontation takes place between the two males. This appears to consist entirely of a display of loud intimidating buzzing, bobbing and hovering accompanied by sudden sideways movements which continue intermittently until one of the males leaves the territory. I have often watched two males in furious encounters of this nature and have never seen them actually make physical contact. It would appear that the whole exercise is one of intimidation only.

A male Carpenter Bee (*Xylocopa* sp.) in full flight.

A male Carpenter Bee on a flower.

A female Carpenter Bee feeding on nectar. Female Carpenter Bees have special compartments on the abdomen in which they carry mites.

Female Carpenter Bees are unique as they have a special chamber on the underside of their abdomens in which they accommodate a number of mites. These mites of the genus *Dinogamasus* are only found in association with the Carpenter Bee and their exact function is not known.

Honey Bees
Family Apidae

Honey Bees are of great economic importance and are legendary for their ability to manufacture considerable quantities of honey from nectar. Other bee species also produce honey but not in significant quantities. Every facet of the biology, behaviour and life cycle of the common Honey Bee (*Apis mellifera*) has been studied in great detail and more has probably been written about the Honey Bee than any other species of insect.

Fact File

- Although when talking of bees one invariably thinks of the Honey Bee, there are, in fact, over 20 000 species of bees in the world.
- Most bees are solitary bees and do not live in beehives as the Honey Bees do.
- Honey Bees are the only insects that produce food for humans.
- Beeswax is secreted by Honey Bees in the form of thin scales. These scales are produced by glands on the underside of the bees' abdomens.

Covered in pollen a Honey Bee digs deep into a flower. Honey Bees are amongst the most important pollinators.

Honey Bees also excel as pollinators. In South Africa the value added to crop production by the commercial pollination of Honey Bees has been estimated to be in the order of R3,2 billion per annum. Wild Honey Bee populations also pollinate as many as 40–70% of indigenous flowering plants.

Contrary to popular belief, the foraging bee seen flitting from flower to flower gathering pollen and nectar does not itself manufacture honey. The nectar it obtains is stored in a special organ called a honey stomach and then carried back to the hive. Here it is transferred to hive workers who convert the nectar to honey by the addition of enzymes.

Lone foraging bees seldom sting if left alone although from time to time an unprovoked attack, at least from a human's point of view, by a single bee may take place. Bees are often drawn to humans through the scent of flower- or fruit-perfumed soaps or shampoos and everyone is familiar with the insistent bees drawn to the rim of a fruit drink or wine glass. The bees are only doing what comes naturally by following a potential food trail and from their perspective you are the intruder.

When certain African species crossbred with European Honey Bees a new strain known as African Killer Bees or Africanised bees resulted. These excessively aggressive bees have caused a high degree of consternation in certain European countries as well as in America where they have launched many unprovoked and deadly attacks on the local inhabitants. These strains appear to be extremely volatile and can be provoked into an attack even by a loud noise. Ongoing precautions are being implemented in an attempt to control the spread of these strains which are also of little use for the production of honey.

When a beehive becomes overpopulated, usually during the spring or early summer, a number of bees which always includes a queen as well as workers and

Deep within an Arum Lily flower a Honey Bee diligently gathers pollen.

drones, leaves the hive to seek a suitable spot on which to establish a new hive. This is called swarming and can consist of anything from 1 000 to 30 000 or more bees moving en masse.

At first they do not move far from the original hive but settle in a convenient spot, sometimes only metres from the hive, while scouts are sent out to find a suitable locality for the establishment of the new hive. They may move to different spots before finally settling but the whole process of swarming is time bound and a matter of urgency as they have no store of food with them and need to start producing as soon as possible.

Swarming bees are said not to be aggressive as they have no hive or young to protect. However, I have no doubt that if they feel their queen is threatened, they will attack to defend her.

Fact File

- A female Honey Bee has a barbed sting which remains behind, resulting in the bee's death as the sting is torn from its body.
- The weather can affect the temper of bees and they are inclined to become more aggressive the higher the temperature. Certain sound frequencies also appear to aggravate them to the point where they could launch an unprovoked attack.

Wasps

Wasps form a large and diverse group in the Hymenoptera Order displaying widely varying habits, behaviour and characteristics. One can, however, broadly divide them into three groups – social wasps, solitary wasps and parasitic wasps.

Social wasps live together with other wasps of the same species in a communal nest, in much the same way as some bees and ants do. Communal nests contain from a few to several hundred wasps with a definite social structure consisting of three castes – the egg-laying queens, workers and males. These nests are nowhere near as large or the social structure as complex as those of ants and many bees.

Solitary wasps do not live in communal nests but can be found nesting independently in the ground. They dig burrows and build cells for their young or construct various types of mud nests according to the specific species. These are attached to surfaces such as trees or masonry.

All solitary wasps provision their cells with food for the young larvae to sustain themselves after they hatch and before the pupation stage. This food consists of live insects that have been stung and paralysed, rendering them incapable of anything but the slightest of movements. Most solitary wasps are highly specialised with regard to the prey that they capture for their young. Some species specialise in bees, some in caterpillars and others in spiders.

The third group are parasitic. They feed on and breed in the bodies, eggs or pupae of other insects. Many of these parasitic wasps are minute in size yet perform valuable services by controlling the populations of other, often harmful, insects.

Several of the parasitic wasps are absolute specialists and parasitise only the larvae or pupae of specific insects, totally ignoring all others. Not all, however, are this fussy and some species parasitise a broad range of insects. Others parasitise plants laying their eggs in the stems, leaves, seeds or flower buds, often causing the formation of galls. There is even a wasp from the Eurytomidae family that parasitises the eggs of Button (Black Widow) spiders.

Paper Wasps
Family Vespidae

There are several species of Paper Wasps that range in size from about 8–38 mm in length. They are usually either reddish, black or brown in colour while some have yellow markings or stripes, usually on the abdomen. Members of the family Vespidae have the ability to fold their wings longitudinally when at rest, a characteristic which can aid in their recognition.

Paper wasps are social insects and live in communal nests consisting of a few to many comb-like cells. These cells are constructed from a papery material produced by chewing up plant fibres.

A single female is responsible for the establishment of a nest. She hunts about for a suitably sheltered nesting site, often in the branches of a tree or under the eaves of a roof. Here she starts her nest by first constructing a flat sheet of pulp and then attaching a number of hexagonal

Paper Wasps (*Belonogaster* sp.) can become highly aggressive. This specimen has clearly been disturbed by the presence of the camera.

A member of the Vespidae family of wasps about to settle on a flower. Note how wasps fly with their legs hanging below the body.

cells to it. She proceeds to lay a single egg in each cell and then diligently guards the nest while waiting for the larvae to hatch. On hatching the young larvae need to be fed and a hectic period lies ahead for the queen female as she has to forage for and masticate countless insects to feed the growing larvae. At the same time she enlarges the cells and expands the nest with new cells in which she again deposits eggs. Only after the larvae have pupated and matured into wasps can she rest and devote herself to full-time egg-laying. The workers now take over the tasks of foraging and enlarging the nest.

Most species of Paper Wasps are well known for their aggressive behaviour and propensity to administer a painful sting. When away from their nest, however, such as when foraging for food, they will seldom bother one. In close proximity to the nest, on the other hand, they become easily provoked and dangerous and will ferociously defend the nest if they feel in any way threatened.

Simply approaching a nest too closely could be considered as threatening while accidentally brushing up against it is a definite reason for reprisal. I have found, when photographing wasps on their nests, that at a certain point they react by lifting their wings in unison. Whether this is in alarm or as a warning I am not sure. Often one wasp leaves the nest and approaches me. I consider this the appropriate time to leave without further delay. Unlike bees, wasps can sting repeatedly and an attack by a nest of Paper Wasps can become an unpleasant experience.

1: A Belonogaster wasp feeding on nectar.
2: The nests of Paper Wasps are made from chewed-up plant fibre which is turned into a paper-like material.
3: Paper Wasps catch insects such as caterpillars and then chew them up finely before taking them to their nest for the young larvae to feed on.
4: A Belonogaster wasp explores the leaves of a succulent plant for caterpillars to take to its larvae in the nest.

Paper Wasps are often found sitting on a flower or a leaf chewing up a caterpillar or other insect. Do not be fooled into thinking it is being eaten. All adult Paper Wasps are vegetarian and feed on nectar or fruit juices. Their larvae, however, are carnivorous and consume a variety of insects which are first macerated and then brought to them by the adults.

Fact File

In the Hymenoptera Order, fertilised eggs produce females while males are produced from unfertilised eggs. As the queen can control whether or not an egg is fertilised, she can therefore also control the ratio of males to females in the nest. In this way she can ensure that a suitable balance is maintained for the proper functioning of the nest.

Above: A Paper Wasp (possibly *Polistes* sp.) explores a flower.
Inset: A Paper Wasp with her newly constructed nest. Eggs have already been laid in three of the cells.

Potter Wasps

Subfamily Eumenidae

Potter or Mason Wasps as they are sometimes called, are solitary wasps belonging to the subfamily Eumenidae. They build mud nests constructed from a mixture of sand, water and saliva. These nests have one to multiple individual cells each containing a single egg. The cells are normally provisioned with larvae or caterpillars that have been paralysed and which will serve as food for the wasp larvae once the eggs hatch.

Nests are typically constructed on plants, trees or walls. Certain species make their nests with elaborate and beautifully formed entrances resembling the neck of a pot or vase, hence the name Potter Wasp. The Potter Wasp lays a single egg, suspending it from the top of the cell by a silken thread where it hangs above its food store until it hatches. Once hatched, the larva falls down on the paralysed caterpillars and proceeds to feed on them.

Like the Vespidae family of wasps the subfamily Eumenidae can also fold their forewings along their length when at rest.

A Potter Wasp (*Delta emarginatum*) rolls a ball of mud which will be used in the building of its nest.

A potter wasp (*Delta* sp.) at a water puddle.

The beautifully vase-shaped nest of a small Potter Wasp attached to the trunk of a tree.

A wasp (*Tricarinodynerus* sp.) explores a wild fruit which it has sensed contains a larva. The spoiled area can be seen on the right side of the fruit.

Moments later the larva is pulled from the fruit. The wasp hops onto a branch where it curls its abdomen around its prey in order to sting and paralyse it.

ANTS, BEES AND WASPS • 75

Fact File

- Fig Wasps (Family Torymidae) are the only insects that can pollinate fig trees.
- Some species of Cuckoo Wasps (Family Chrysididae) invade the nests of other wasps or bees, kill the larvae they find and deposit their own eggs in the nests.
- Many wasps parasitise other insects, such as moths and butterflies, by laying their eggs in or on the host's larvae.
- Wasps are important bio-control agents as they play a vital role in controlling the numbers of many other insects.

The striking yellow and black *Delta lepeleterii* wasp collects water for mixing mud for construction of its nest.

Mud Wasps and Sand Wasps
Family Sphecidae

Like Potter Wasps, Mud Wasps also construct their nests from a mixture of mud and water. These can easily be differentiated from the finely worked vase-like nests of those built by the Eumenidae as they often end up as rather large packs of mud stuck up against a wall or tree or on a rock. Each construction usually contains a number of individual sausage-like cells which are stocked with paralysed spiders and then covered over once again with mud.

The Sand Wasps dig nests in the ground using their forelegs which are equipped with sand rakes for this purpose. They sink a tunnel of about 50–60 cm running down at an angle and then clear a chamber for a number of individual cells. Depending on the specific species, these cells may be stocked with caterpillars, flies, bees or other insects. Unlike the Potter Wasps or Mud Wasps, many of the Sand Wasps do not immediately seal their nests but as the larvae grow they replenish the food store from time to time by bringing in fresh insects.

A Mud Dauber Wasp (*Sceliphron spirifex*) on the hunt. These wasps capture and provision their nests with spiders.

The roughly built nest of a Mud Wasp containing a number of individual cells.

The inside of a Mud Wasp's nest shows a number of pupae casings and the remains of a spider meal.

A Sand Wasp (*Bembix* sp.) clearing away the entrance to her nest.

A wasp (possibly the Thread-waisted Wasp, *Ammophila* sp.) catching a caterpillar much larger than itself. The wasp had great difficulty in lifting the caterpillar and proceeded to drag it along the ground.

ANTS, BEES AND WASPS • 77

Parasitic wasps

A significant number of wasp species from different families such as the Ichneumonidae, Braconidae and Chalcididae among others, parasitise a variety of other arthropods, pupae and larvae as well as plants. Some lay their eggs either on or in the bodies of caterpillars or the pupae of moths and butterflies. In some cases the newly hatched wasp larva continues to live in the body of its host, slowly devouring it from the inside until the host dies and the wasp is ready to emerge.

The tiny *Brachymeria kassalensis* wasp, a member of the Family Chalcididae specifically parasitises the pupae of the Garden Acraea Butterfly (*Acraea horta*). The wasp undergoes its full cycle from egg through larva and pupa to adult in the butterfly pupa before it chews its way out.

A tiny wasp (possibly *Braconid* sp.) of only about 4 mm in length settles on a flower, its semi-transparent wings breaking the light up into a spectrum of colours.

Left: A metallic green Cuckoo Wasp from the family Chrysididae. These wasps, like cuckoo birds, lay their eggs in the nests of other wasps and bees.
Right: What appears to be a small Braconid wasp. Braconids parasitise the larvae of various other insects.

The tiny parasitic Chalcidid wasps, which measure only 6–7 mm when fully grown, belong to the Chalcididae family. The *Brachymeria kassalensis* shown here specialises in parasitising the chrysalis of the Acraea butterflies on which it feeds as a larva.

1: The young adult parasitic wasp has started eating its way out from an Acraea chrysalis hanging from a tree trunk. It is a slow and arduous task as the dry, hard shell of the chrysalis is broken away piece by tiny piece and it is carried out with frequent rests in between. At this stage the wasp has also just recently emerged from its own pupa and is still relatively weak.

2: The wasp has now already managed to extract its head and forelegs. However, the opening is still too small to allow the rest of its body to exit. It will have to withdraw again and enlarge the opening. This process of attempting to exit and then again having to go back was repeated four times before the little wasp was able to extract itself with great difficulty from the shell.

3: Three quarters of the way out and almost there. All that was needed now was brute strength combined with numerous contortions to free the pair of enlarged hind legs (femora), which is characteristic of these wasps.

4: Free at last from the chrysalis shell, the wasp rests to regain its strength and stretch its wings before flying off. The whole process from opening up the tiny hole to fully emerging from the chrysalis took more than three hours.

A brightly coloured *Archibracon servillei* wasp (Braconidae family) with characteristically long antennae.

A Citrus Swallowtail (*Papilio demodocus*) settles on a daisy in search of a meal in late afternoon sunshine, unaware that its every move is being recorded by the camera.

Butterflies and Moths
Order Lepidoptera

The name Lepidoptera is a combination of the Greek words "lepido" which means scale and "ptera" meaning wings. The name refers to the fact that the wings of the adult insects are covered by flattened hairs or scales.

Butterflies are probably the most loved insects in the world. Admired for their beauty and spectacular colours, they have captured the imagination of artists, designers and stylists in every field of creativity while also holding a distinct and often revered place in folklore, myth and legend. Fossil evidence suggests that butterflies date back at least 40–50 million years.

Several butterfly species are habitat dependent, some can survive only under certain environmental conditions and others require certain host plants on which to feed and breed. The specific conditions required by many butterflies serve to make them valuable environmental indicators, as a decrease in particular butterfly populations in a given area points to the existence of environmental problems or change. One such butterfly is South Africa's Roodepoort Copper Butterfly (*Aloeides dentatis*) which is endemic only to the Ruimsig area of Roodepoort in Gauteng and where a reserve has been set up specially to protect it. Another is the Brenton Blue (*Orachrysops niobe*) which can only be found in a particular area near Knysna.

The study and practice of collecting butterflies is called lepidoptery. It is a popular hobby and amateur lepidopterists often make valuable contributions to the discovery and identification of new species of butterfly. Unfortunately, however, the collection of rare and endangered butterflies poses a real danger to the survival of many of these species as they are removed from their natural habitats to feed an ever-expanding international trade where many are sold for exorbitant prices.

In contrast with the flamboyant butterflies, their rather drab relatives, the moths, are often scorned and generally seen as pests. The differences between butterflies and moths are small and sometimes indistinct with some butterfly families having characteristics normally associated with moths and vice versa. The Skipper Butterfly (Family Hesperiidae), for example, has a bulky body that more resembles the body of a moth than a butterfly. On the other hand, not all moths are drab. Many species are as large as the average butterfly and show equally vivid colouration with intricate wing markings such as eyespots and colour patterns.

Butterflies normally rest with wings folded above the body although some do sometimes sit with wings outspread.

A Citrus Swallowtail butterfly displays its tightly coiled proboscis.

Moths are not capable of keeping their wings folded above the body and normally rest with them roof-like over the body or spread alongside the body.

Although many exceptions do apply the following can be used as a general guide for the novice to the differences and similarities between the two groups:

- **Antennae:** A butterfly's antennae end in a knob or club and may also be curved or hooked at the tip while a moth's antennae are simple and hair-like in females and heavy and comb-like or feathery in males.
- **Wings:** Both butterflies and moths have large wings which are covered in innumerable small scales, frequently in characteristic patterns. When at rest a moth folds its wings across its back. A butterfly brings its wings together above the back.
- **Body:** Moths are generally heavy-bodied while butterflies are thin-bodied.
- **Nocturnal or diurnal:** Butterflies tend to fly mainly by day and moths by night, although there are some moths that fly by day.
- **Pupation:** Moths pupate underground or in a cocoon which is spun by the moth caterpillar (larva) while butterflies do not spin cocoons but develop in a chrysalis which is usually attached to a twig, leaf or plant stem.
- **Feeding:** Both butterflies and moths feed by sipping nectar using a long coiled proboscis. Some moths do not feed at all and have a reduced or no proboscis. A few primitive moths have mandibles for chewing instead of a proboscis. There are also butterflies that are predacious and feed on small bugs such as the plant hoppers.

There is little to differentiate between the caterpillars (larvae) of butterflies and moths. Caterpillars can be either smooth or hairy while some may have tufts of coloured hair or bristles. Some have barbed hairs containing toxins capable of inflecting painful burns. They do not have wings but move about on three pairs of jointed or true

A beautiful little Geranium Bronze butterfly (*Cacyreus* sp.) shows off its knobbed antennae.

> ### Fact File
> - Some moths are just as beautiful and colourful as butterflies while others are drab and grey.
> - Both moths and butterflies go through a larva or caterpillar stage before achieving adulthood.

legs and up to five pairs of fleshy, unjointed prolegs. The prolegs have small hooks called crochets that help them cling to surfaces. The last pair of prolegs called claspers is found at the rear of the abdomen. This pair is usually thicker than the others.

> ### FACT FILE
> In flight, the front and hindwings of Lepidoptera are linked together by a bristle (frenulum) or a membranous flap (jugum) so that both wings move up and down in synchrony.

The prolegs disappear during pupation and the adult insect is left with only the six jointed legs. In one family, the Nymphalidae, the first pair of true legs is greatly reduced to small brush-like organs and is non-functional as walking legs. Members of this family are commonly called Brush-footed Butterflies.

All caterpillars have chewing mouthparts in contrast to adult butterflies or moths which have sucking mouthparts. Most caterpillars are vegetarians and throughout their cycle do little but eat, building up energy for the pupation stage. They stop only to moult, shedding their skins as they grow. This happens several times during their life cycle. The stage between each moult is called an instar. In many cases, such as with the cut-worm, green loopers or bollworm, the larvae are better known than the actual adult moth or butterfly.

There are an estimated 165 000 different species of butterflies and moths worldwide of which the greater majority are moths. South Africa has just over 600 species of butterflies.

The wings of butterflies and moths are made up of millions of minute scales attached to the wing membrane and easily come off as a white powder if the wings are touched. Colour patterns, such as the eyespots found on many butterflies and moths, are made up of these scales. Each scale has its own colour and fit together like tiles in a mosaic.

A moth pupa hangs suspended on a twig. Some moth species leave protective hairs from their larvae embedded in their cocoons or pupae.

BUTTERFLIES
SWALLOWTAILS AND ORANGE DOGS
FAMILY PAPILIONIDAE

The Citrus Swallowtail (*Papilio demodocus*) is also known as the Christmas Butterfly. This beautiful, large, black and yellow/white butterfly has eyespots on the front and rear of the hindwings. It is found throughout the country during late spring and summer in flower beds or on flowering shrubs where it feeds on nectar.

Its larvae are remarkable as during the early stages of their development, they resemble bird droppings and can thus easily be overlooked when stationary on a leaf or twig. The larvae later develop into large green caterpillars with white, brown and black body markings.

A full view of the Citrus Swallowtail showing its white (sometimes yellow) spotted wings and prominent coloured eyespots. This large butterfly with a wingspan of just over 80 mm is also known as the Christmas Butterfly.

The caterpillar of the Citrus Swallowtail is green with, black, brown and white markings which run across the body. These caterpillars can be a pest on young citrus plants.

When threatened, the caterpillar will rear up and display its red fork-like osmeterium. It is also capable of exuding a foul smell.

This mature caterpillar is preparing for pupation by starting to spin silk threads which will eventually form a pad to which the pupa will adhere.

The chrysalis of a Citrus Swallowtail stuck to a twig at the bottom and supported by a silken halter. It will hang in this position until the adult butterfly emerges from the chrysalis.

A newly emerged butterfly clings firmly to its pupal case.

Only once the wings have expanded and stiffened, a process achieved by pumping body fluid into the veins of the wings, can the butterfly attempt to fly.

The caterpillars are commonly known as Orange Dogs. When threatened, they rear up by lifting the front part of the body. At the same time they extend a bright red-orange forked-shaped organ called an osmeterium from the segment just behind the head. The osmeterium is then ominously waved about in the air. The caterpillar can also emit an obnoxious smell, thus further discouraging any potential enemy.

Orange Dogs are often found on citrus trees. Should you encounter one, take a stiff blade of grass or a soft small twig and gently stroke it along the body. This will be enough to cause it to react and extend its osmeterium.

The larval stage lasts approximately a month. The caterpillar then attaches itself to a twig by means of a silk thread that it spins and changes into a chrysalis. At first the chrysalis is a leaf-green colour but gradually darkens to brown as it ages. In about 10 to 14 days, depending on the prevailing climatic conditions, the adult butterfly emerges. From my experience this usually takes place early in the morning.

The pupa splits on the upper side and the butterfly, with wings folded tightly against its body, tentatively makes its way out, leaving the thin pupal skin behind. At this stage it cannot fly and clings to the pupal skin as it slowly begins to expand its wings. Body fluid is pumped into the wing veins and the wings are opened to stiffen and dry. The butterfly also begins to move cautiously about, repeatedly flexing its wings and clinging tenaciously to the surrounding foliage as it makes its way to a high point. Suddenly it launches itself and takes to the air as if it had been flying all its life. The task ahead – to find a mate and by doing so ensure the survival of its species.

Garden Acraea
Family Nymphalidae

The black-dotted, red to orange-coloured Garden Acraea Butterfly (*Acraea* sp.) with its semi-transparent forewings is found in abundance in gardens and woodlands throughout the moister regions of the country. Its strongly contrasting colours act as a warning to predators that it should be left alone as it is poisonous.

As a larva it feeds mainly on grenadilla plants (Passifloraceae) and Wild Peach (*Kiggelaria africana*) from which it builds highly distasteful toxic compounds that can result in the death of a predator such as a bird. Consequently, the larvae of these butterflies can move about and feed with impunity as no predator will touch them. These toxins are retained in the body throughout pupation and remain present when the insect reaches its adult butterfly stage.

The black, red and yellow pupae of the Garden Acraea can frequently be seen hanging upside down on tree trunks, plants or walls. These pupae are often parasitised by tiny chalcidid wasps which then develop within the pupa, killing it in the process. When fully developed the wasp cuts a neat hole in the chrysalis to exit.

The striking Acraea butterfly has dotted hindwings while the upper part of the forewings are transparent. Here it can be seen with proboscis deeply inserted into a flower as it sips nectar.

Above: Small Orange Acraea (*Hyalites eponina*).

Top right: The chrysalis of the Acraea is usually attached to plants or branches but can also often be seen on brick or concrete walls. The chrysalis may be parasitised by wasps.

Bottom right: When seen from the top the Acraea is a brilliant orange. Its bright colours are a warning to predators that it is poisonous.

SULPHURS AND WHITES
FAMILY PIERIDAE

The butterflies of this family are mainly white and yellow coloured, sometimes with orange patches or black edges to the wings, and often with black spots. Many of the species are sexually dimorphic so members of the same species look different depending on their sex. This difference between the sexes is often apparent in the pattern or number of black spots on the wings.

Some species are also seasonally variable showing differences between individuals emerging during a wet or dry period. Many of the Pieridae have ultraviolet patterns and markings on the wings that are invisible to the human eye but can be seen by their own sort and that apparently play an important role in courtship.

Adults of all species can often be seen flying rapidly and erratically amongst plants visiting flowers for nectar or patrolling in search of receptive mates.

Magnificent against a contrasting black background of dark foliage, a yellow and orange Dotted Border butterfly (*Mylothris* sp.) rests on a twig.

Broad-bordered Grass Yellow (*Eurema brigitta brigitta*).

Left: A Grass Yellow (*Eurema* sp.) explores a muddy patch. These dainty little butterflies will usually be found close to or on the ground.

Right: Brown-veined White (*Belenois* sp.). Found throughout the country, these butterflies sometimes migrate in great numbers during the summer.

Skippers
Family Hesperiidae

This family contains the group of butterflies generally known as Skippers. The name is derived from the rapid and often erratic way that they fly, skipping as it were from flower to flower.

When at rest some species adopt a distinctive position with the forewings open half-way and the hindwings fully open while others rest with their wings completely flat. They can often be seen moving about at dusk and some even fly at night.

A Skipper butterfly commonly known as a Policeman explores a flower. The rather drab coloured skippers are very moth-like in appearance. Notice also the curved ends to its antennae.

In contrast to other butterflies, they have heavy, hairy bodies and are almost moth-like in general appearance. Although there are exceptions, most members of this family are rather drab and do not display anywhere near the range of vibrant colours found in most other families. They can also be recognised by their antennae which are curved or hook-like at the tips.

> **FACT FILE**
> - Butterflies rest with their wings folded vertically above the body. Moths' wings often form a roof over the body.
> - Butterflies have long thin antennae ending in clubs or knobs. Moths' antennae are thread-like or feather-like without a club.

YELLOW PANSY
FAMILY NYMPHALIDAE

Its vibrant yellow, orange and blue patches on a black background make the Yellow Pansy Butterfly (*Junonia hierta*) an instant eye catcher when in flight or feeding with its wings open. The underside of the wings, in contrast, are a rather drab grey which belies its true beauty. The Yellow Pansy is a widespread species which can often be found feeding in flower beds or resting on moist ground.

Right: The drab grey on the underside of the Yellow Pansy belies the richness of the colours on its upper side.
Below left: A Yellow Pansy (*Junonia hierta*) shows off its brilliantly coloured patterned wings while perching open-winged on a plant.
Below right: A Yellow Pansy launches itself from a flower head.

Painted Lady
Family Nymphalidae

The Painted Lady (*Cynthia cardui*, also known as *Vanessa cardui*) is a delightful multi-coloured butterfly found throughout South Africa and is also considered to be one of the most common and widely distributed butterflies worldwide. It can normally be seen throughout the year, sometimes in large numbers.

Right: The beautiful little Painted Lady (*Cynthia cardui*).
Below: A Painted Lady feeding.

African Monarch
Family Nymphalidae

The African Monarch (*Danaus chrysippus*) is a large, slow-flying butterfly of a group known as Brush-footed Butterflies. The name is derived from the fact that the first two legs of these butterflies are greatly reduced and look like brushes. They are of no use for walking and the insect thus in effect has only four walking legs.

African Monarchs are found throughout the country, frequenting gardens where they are found sipping from flowers. They fly from dawn to dusk and can be seen late in the day fluttering low over bushes to find a resting place for the night.

Their larvae feed on milkweed, hence their alternate name of Milkweed Butterflies. Both the larvae and the adults carry an accumulation of toxic substances in their bodies which they have obtained from the milkweed host plant and which makes them distasteful or poisonous to predators. Their bright contrasting colouration acts as a warning sign and potential predators soon learn to avoid them.

In addition to their toxicity, these butterflies also have a tough, leathery skin that makes it possible for them to survive an occasional attack should it occur. If attacked, a monarch will fake death while at the same time emitting a nauseating liquid that encourages the predator to promptly release it.

African Monarch butterfly (*Danaus chrysippus*) feeding.

Coppers and Blues
Family Lycaenidae

This large family of butterflies is said to represent about 40% of all butterfly species. It contains the Gossamer-winged Butterflies, Coppers, Hairstreaks, Harvesters and Blues. Many of them are unique as their larvae live together with ants. While ants attack most insect larvae, the larvae of many of the Lycaenidae family have glands that secrete a honeydew that appears to both attract and subdue the ants.

Most of the Lycaenidae are small, brightly coloured and have tails which look almost like antennae. Together with the eyespots on their wings these serve to confuse potential predators as to which is, in fact, their front and back ends.

A tiny Geranium Bronze butterfly (*Cacyreus marshalli*) displays its antennae-like tails and eyespot. They often sit with their rear end raised to confuse potential predators.

The "antennae" mimicking tails and the eyespots are clearly visible on this magnificent Common Hairtail butterfly (*Athene definita definita*).

A dainty little butterfly from the Lycaenidae family. Many of these little beauties have a total wingspan of 24 mm or less.

Moths
Bagworms
Family Psychidae

Bagworms are well known for their protective silken larval cases covered by a sundry assortment of twigs, leaves, debris and grass stalks. These bags can be up to 50 mm long and are typically found hanging from twigs, often in acacia or wattle trees. These trees provide food for the Wattle Bagworm, one of the best known of the somewhat 30 species found in South Africa.

Shortly after hatching, a Bagworm starts to build its case by spinning threads of strong silk to which it attaches pieces of vegetation. During the early stages of its development the larva is mobile and moves about by dragging its twig-encrusted case behind it. As it grows, it expands its case by adding new material to the front until a point is reached where the case is permanently attached to a twig or branch. Here the larva pupates in the case, after which the adult male moth flies off in search of a suitable mating partner. He has very little time to do this as the lifespan of an adult moth is only a few days.

The maggot-like adult female Bagworm Moth has no legs, wings or eyes and never leaves the case where she awaits the arrival of a male. After mating, she lays her eggs and dies.

A Bagworm larval case. The female bagworm spends her entire life in the case and never leaves. After mating she lays eggs and then dies.

Bagworm larva. The larva drags its case behind it. When it reaches maturity it will fasten the case to a twig and withdraw to pupate.

Owl Moths
Family Noctuidae

The Owl Moths are large to very large, impressive brownish moths with large prominent eyespots on the forewings, from which they derive their name. They are night-flying but are also attracted to lights and may thus frequently be found indoors quietly sitting against a wall or curtains.

It is also not unusual to have an Owl Moth casually settle on a wine glass during a braai in the bushveld, as they have a particular liking for alcohol and are strongly attracted by alcoholic drinks or fermenting fruits.

Fact File

Some caterpillars use "ballooning" to transport themselves to new locations. A silk thread is released by the caterpillar and picked up by the wind, carrying the caterpillar with it.

A Wavy Owl Moth (*Calliodes pretiosissima*) displays the striking eyespots from which its name is derived.

A Cream-striped Owl Moth (*Cyligramma latona*) clings to the bark of a tree.

Plume Moths
Family Pterophoridae

The plume moth is one of those extraordinary creations often found in nature. One could not be blamed for passing them by without ever realising that they are in fact moths.

Like other moths they have only two pairs of wings, but these have been unusually modified. Each wing has been divided into two or more spars with what appear to be dishevelled bristles trailing at the ends.

They rest with wings extended and rolled up to form a T-shape which makes them look very much like a dried blade of grass or a rolled-up dead leaf.

Plume moth (possibly *Agdistis* sp.) clings to a plant stem with plumed wings rolled up to form a "T" shape.

A Plume Moth displays its many spined legs against a colourful background.

CRIMSON-SPECKLED FOOTMAN
FAMILY AGARISTIDAE

The Crimson-speckled Footman (*Utetheisa pulchella*) is a colourful, medium-sized moth characterised by its crimson and black spotted wings. The Footman is found throughout South Africa. It flies by day or night but can generally more often be seen during daylight hours where it will be found resting on low vegetation or visiting flowers in search of nectar.

A multi-coloured Crimson-speckled Footman (*Utetheisa pulchella*) sucking nectar from a flower.

Hawk Moths
Family Sphingidae

Hawk moths are medium to large moths, also commonly known as Sphinx Moths. Most have a characteristic arrow-like shape as a result of their long, narrow forewings which are considerably larger than the hindwings. The body of a Hawk Moth is tapered toward the back and has a distinctly cigar-shaped appearance. The abdomen of some species is adorned with stripes or bands.

With some exceptions, Hawk Moths generally only fly at night although they can often be seen at dusk searching for nectar.

1: The Oleander Hawk Moth (*Daphnis nerii*) is olive green, patterned in pink with deep red eyes.
2: African Humming Bird Moth (*Macroglossum trochilus*).
3: A Hawk Moth (possibly the Mulberry Hawk, *Pseudoclanis postica*). These moths tend to rest by day but can often be seen flying from dusk onwards.
4: Silver-striped Hawk Moth (*Hippotion celerio*).

Oleander Hawk Moth

The Oleander Hawk Moth (*Daphnis nerii*) is a large, rather impressive moth with a wingspan in excess of 100 mm. Green in colour overall, the body and wings vary from deep olive green in some parts to a greenish white in others. The wings are adorned with wavy lines and patterns in eye-catching pink edged by white. Most striking of all, however, are its eyes of deep ruby red.

African Humming Bird Moth

The African Humming Bird Moth is a day-flying member of the Hawk Moth family. It can hover in one place like a helicopter, wings beating at a tremendous rate but otherwise it remains quite stationary. As the name implies, it is reminiscent of a miniature hummingbird. It feeds by extending its exceptionally long proboscis to extract nectar from flowers.

Fact File
- Certain caterpillars can "hear" sound by means of the fine hairs on their bodies.
- The hearing organs of moths are found on their abdomen, thorax and even on their front wings in some species.

An African Humming Bird Moth hovers while sipping nectar from a flower with its extraordinarily long proboscis.

Clear-wing Moths
Family Sesiidae

These little daylight-flying moths are unusual as parts, or in some species, the whole of their wings lack the closely-packed scales normally found on the wings of moths. This absence of covering scales shows as transparent areas on the wings, hence the name Clear-wing.

Many Clear-wing Moths are also convincing bee or wasp mimics, some with elongated wasp-like bodies adorned with yellow stripes.

The larvae of several of these moths are wood boring and attack a variety of shrubs and trees, including various fruit trees.

A tiny Clear-wing Moth hangs upside-down from the underside of a leaf.

Golden Plusia
Family Noctuidae

Found throughout the country, the Golden Plusia (*Trichoplusia orichalcea*) is easily recognised by the beautiful metallic golden triangles resembling fine gold foil on the brownish background of the forewings. The larvae of these moths, which are called semi-loopers, can be destructive to a number of vegetable crops such as lettuce and various legumes although its natural food plant is the blackjack.

Above: The Golden Plusia (*Trichoplusia orichalcea*) gets its name from the gold foil-like patches on the forewings.

Left: A Golden Plusia moth feeding. This moth is seldom seen with its wings spread, as it prefers sitting with wings held roof-like over the body and forelegs stretched out in front.

Fig-tree Moth
Family Lymantriidae

Covered in fine, silver-tinged white hairs, the Fig-tree Moth (*Naroma varipes*) appears almost fluffy and cuddly. Like all members of the Lymantriidae family, which also includes Tussock and Gypsy moths, the mouthparts of Fig-tree Moths do not function and the adult moths do not feed. As the name implies, the larvae feed on fig trees.

The larvae of most of the members of this family have tufts of barbed stinging hairs which are also embedded in the cocoons that they spin, usually to be found at the bases of the trees on which they feed. Males of the Lymantriidae family have large, handsome antennae.

A Fig-tree Moth shows off its magnificent pair of plumose antennae.

Fig-tree Moth (*Naroma varipes*). The larvae of this moth feed on fig trees, hence its common name.

CATERPILLARS

No discussion on the Lepidotera Order would be complete without reference to the larvae or, as they are more commonly known, the caterpillars of the family. During this stage of the life cycle of both butterflies and moths, which can last from weeks to months, caterpillars consume vast quantities of vegetation. They grow at a fast rate, their bodies expanding in a balloon-like fashion. During their lifespan they moult four or five times before pupating. Their voracious appetite serves to make many of them serious agricultural pests. In spite of this, many are striking and magnificent creatures in their own right.

Let's take the caterpillar of the Cabbage-tree Emperor Moth (*Bunaea alcinoe*), a member of the Saturniidae

Striking to look at but a pest. The Yellow and Black Banded Lily Borer from the family Noctuidae causes considerable damage to plants by boring into their stems.

A Cabbage-tree Emperor Moth (*Bunaea alcinoe*) larva hangs by its claspers from the branches of a cabbage-tree (Kiepersol).

Family, as an example. Thick as a man's finger and 100 mm long, it feeds on the leaves of the Cabbage-tree (*Cussonia*, Kiepersol). An infestation of these caterpillars is capable of totally defoliating a large tree before they fall to the ground where they bury themselves to pupate. Normally the tree survives this drastic pruning, although I have seen trees die after a severe attack by Emperor Moth caterpillars.

The caterpillar has a deep mat-black body with sharp, white, porcupine-like spikes which, although they appear intimidating, are soft and incapable of piercing the human skin. These are interspersed along the length of the body with large bright orange spots. It is an awe-inspiring creature when seen for the first time.

Other large and attention-grabbing caterpillars are those of the Hawk Moths (Family Sphingidae). Many have either pointed or curved horns on their tails, very small heads in comparison to the size of their bodies and large prominent eyespots. They feed on a variety of vegetation. Anyone who has arum lilies in their garden will no doubt be familiar with at least one or more of the Hawk Moth caterpillars as they can decimate a patch of these plants in no time.

Although most caterpillars are considerably smaller and so not quite as noticeable as those of

Newly hatched larvae of the Emperor Moth. They have only one purpose in life – to eat. These larvae are capable of totally stripping a tree of its leaves in a short time.

The Kiepersol or Cabbage-tree (*Cussonia paniculata*) on which the Emperor Moths feed.

A Hawk Moth caterpillar (family Sphingidae). It has a pointed horn on the tail, 10 prolegs and three pairs of true legs, which are very small and insignificant in relation to its body size.

A closer look at the Hawk Moth caterpillar showing its very small head and large black and yellow eyespot intended to intimidate predators.

Caterpillars come in many guises: some are smooth, others hairy, some sting and some don't but all at a later stage in their life cycles will change into either a butterfly or a moth. Caterpillars are so many and varied that the only sure way of identifying many of them is to wait and see what the adult form looks like.

the two families mentioned above, many are equally interesting in structure and appearance and each one remains uniquely fascinating. Some are smooth and soft, others may be hairy and often flamboyant with tufts or brushes of coloured hairs or spines. Many have stinging hairs which are hollow, quill-like and connected to poison sacs that release chemical toxins capable of inflicting painful burns on the human skin.

Stinging caterpillars are usually brightly coloured to warn predators of the impending danger. Despite this, they can very easily be overlooked among foliage. Anyone who has accidentally brushed against a bush or shrub infested with these caterpillars will attest to the intense pain caused by contact with their spines. So powerful is the toxin they release, that it is unnecessary for the spines to pierce the skin – just the lightest contact is sufficient to release the poison and cause burns.

A bright yellow Ten-spotted Leaf Beetle (*Cryptocephalus decemnotatus*) on a crimson flower. Size 6 mm.

Beetles
Order Coleoptera

The Greek words "koleos" (sheath) and "ptera" (wings) are combined to form the word, Coleoptera, which refers to the sheath-like front wings that cover and protect the delicate membranous hindwings of beetles.

The large and diverse Order Coleoptera contains all the beetles of which there are more than 350 000 known species worldwide. Beetles, in fact, make up 40% of all living insects. They show extreme diversity in appearance, general form, habitat and choice of food. In size they vary from a minute 0,25 mm up to almost 180 mm in length while in colour they can be anything from dull grey to bright green, yellow, red or a combination of various colour patterns. Some beetles are so beautifully and vibrantly coloured that for centuries they have been used as subjects for jewellery. They are also the favourites of collectors who are often prepared to pay exorbitant prices for rare and exotic specimens.

Beetles are unique as their forewings have evolved into hard protective shields or wing cases without any veins, called elytra. Although many insects have adapted forewings, beetles are the only insects with true elytra. A second

Camouflage plays an important role for many insects in the fight for survival. Here a Long-horn Beetle (*Phryneta spinator*) blends in with a background of bark.

Predacious Black Mealy Bug (*Exochomus flavipes*).

Even bugs have bugs – a Scarab beetle infected with parasitic mites!

pair of membranous wings, if present, is used for flying. However, not all beetles can fly as in some species the elytra are fused together, while others have no flying wings at all.

All beetles have chewing mouthparts which are adapted in various ways to allow them to feed on other insects, wood, fruit, nectar, fungi, leaves or other plant material.

While certain species such as the dung beetle are beneficial to humans, others can be highly destructive pests and cause considerable damage to stored foods, forests, ornamental plants and various crops.

Several beetles interact with other insects such as bees, ants or termites in symbiotic relationships. Such beetles frequently live in the nests of these insects and are protected and fed by their hosts.

Fact File

As adults, most beetles have a hard, dense exoskeleton that covers and protects most of their body surface. The front wings, called elytra, are just as hard as the rest of the exoskeleton. They fold down over the abdomen and serve as protective covers for the large, membranous hindwings.

Fruit Chafer (*Leucocelis* sp.).

Fact File

Coleoptera is the largest order in the animal kingdom. It includes 40% of all insects and nearly 30% of all animal species.

Top: Fool's Gold Beetle (*Aspidimorpha tecta*). This little leaf beetle from the family Chrysomelidae reminds one of a miniature golden tortoise. It feeds on foliage and is particularly partial to the Morning Glory plant.

Above: This little Rose Beetle of the Scarabaeidae family has a finely pitted pronotum and pitted and lined elytra.

The Carrion beetle (*Thanatophilus mutilatus*) lives on the flesh of dead animals.

Below: Zig-zag Fruit Chafer (*Anisorrhina flavomaculata*) on fruit. There are various small colour variations of this species, even in the same area.

The beautifully sculptured elytra of the Amethyst Fruit Chafer (*Leucocelis amethystina*). This clearly shows how the two "wings" of the elytra meet in the middle.

CMR beetle (*Mylabris oculata*) in flight. The elytra have been lifted to allow use of the delicate flying wings.

Close-up of a Fork-horned Rhino Beetle from the subfamily Dynastinae.

An adult Fork-horned Beetle has both horn-like processes on the pronotum as well as an impressive forked horn on the head (*Cyphonistes vallatus*).

Dung Beetles
Family Scarabaeidae

The humble Dung Beetles, often depicted rolling their balls of dung along, fulfil a beneficial agricultural and ecological function. They perform the indispensable but unenviable task of breaking up, dispersing and burying dung which would lie unattended in the wild without their help. They belong to the Family Scarabaeidae which ironically also includes the Fruit Chafer and Flower Chafer Beetles, so well known for decimating our rose bushes and other ornamental plants.

There are approximately 8 000 species of Dung Beetles. Wherever cattle, horses or wild animals are found, Dung Beetles will also be found. The dung which the beetles so industriously gather, transport, fight about

A Dung Beetle rolls its ball over rough terrain. In its eagerness to gather a sufficient supply of dung a beetle will often roll a ball much larger than it can handle.

A profile of the large *Heliocopris* beetle showing the impressive horns and projections on the pronotum and head.

and breed in contains large quantities of hugely nutritious material which supports the dung beetles throughout their life cycles.

Although best known for their ball-rolling activities, not all dung beetles roll dung balls. Some species dig a chamber directly under a dung patty into which they then shovel the dung. This dung-filled chamber is also where they lay their eggs. There are other species which feed on the surface and do not bury the dung at all.

The ball-rolling species use their strong legs to compact and form round balls of dung which vary in size from as large as a tennis ball to relatively small depending on the specific species. These dung balls are often rolled considerable distances away before being buried. Their determination in executing this task is admirable. Working tirelessly, often in male and female pairs, they navigate various obstacles such as rocks, gullies and undergrowth until they reach a suitable spot. I have often observed them as they try over and over again to mount an incline or get through a furrow only to have the dung ball, to which they doggedly attempt to cling, repeatedly roll back, often throwing them onto their backs.

Members of the Scarabaeidae family can always be recognised by their lamellate antenna, which consists of a number of plates that can be opened and closed, like a fan.

Dung beetles have specially adapted forelegs used for digging and scraping. The forelegs are also without a tarsus (foot).

Dung beetles (*Heliocopris* sp.).

Small green Dung Beetle (possibly *Garetta* sp.).

When eventually a suitable spot is reached, they start digging using their specially adapted forelegs. Once the dung ball has been safely buried, mating takes place and some of the dung is eaten. The rest is used to form smaller balls into which eggs are laid. After hatching, the larvae feed on their brood ball until they change into pupae and later into beetles.

Fact File

- All Dung Beetles are scarabs, that is, members of the Scarabaeidae Family of beetles.
- The large *Heliocopris* species with a body length of about 50 mm is commonly encountered on the South African veld or wherever horses, cattle or game are to be found.
- Males of some scarabs often have prominent horns on the head and pronotum. These are used for defending their territory or dung balls against other invading males but may also be of significance during courting rituals.

Long-horn Beetles
Family Cerambycidae

Long-horn Beetles can easily be recognised by their extremely long antennae, which in some species often exceed twice the length of the insect's body. Adult beetles feed mainly on flowers, leaves and bark.

The larvae are mostly wood borers and can be serious pests in timber trees and wood including wooden houses and wood products. On the other hand, the larvae also perform a valuable task in breaking down dead trees and facilitating nutrient recycling in forest ecosystems.

As the larvae tunnel their way deep into timber they are seldom seen but the adult beetles can often be found on flowers or foliage. Their lengthy and in several species rather flamboyant antennae make them striking insects that seldom escape detection.

Fact File
- Many Long-horn Beetles are wood boring. However, nearly all attack only dead or dying trees and consequently perform a valuable task in breaking down dead wood.
- The name is derived from the long antennae which are often longer than the entire body.

A Phoracantha Longhorn (*Phoracantha* sp.). Originally from Australia, the larva of this beetle feeds on eucalypt trees. Body length 16 mm; antennae 22 mm.

Left: A longhorn beetle displaying its antennae as it moves across the surface of a leaf. Body length 10 mm.

Below: With its antennae swaying alertly a Brown Longhorn Beetle makes its way up a dead twig (*Macrotoma* sp.).

1: A Pondo-Pondo Longhorn Beetle (*Ceroplesis* sp.) with a magnificent pair of antennae. While this specimen had a body length of 30 mm, the antennae measured 35 mm.

2: The Metallic Longhorn Beetle (*Promeces longipes*) is often found on flowers. Body length 13 mm (excluding antennae).

3: A metallic blue Longhorn Beetle with colourfully banded antennae and swollen blue femora.

4: This handsome little Longhorn Beetle could possibly be *Tragocephala* sp.

The Fig Tree Borer Longhorn Beetle (*Phryneta spinator*) is a serious pest of fig trees. It lays its eggs in a small slit that it makes near the base of a branch. When the larvae hatch they bore into the tree and feed on both bark and wood, forming tunnels in the wood as they do so. Larvae can take from 2 to 3 years to develop resulting in considerable damage or death to the tree.

LADYBIRDS
FAMILY COCCINELLIDAE

The familiar little round-bodied beetles fondly known as Ladybirds are as a rule welcomed in gardens as friends of the gardener and allies in the fight against pests such as plant lice (aphids). The adult beetles are typically colourful with yellow, red or black bodies which are often multi-coloured or spotted while the larvae are black with yellow or white markings and often have spines.

Throughout their life cycle, Ladybirds make a valuable contribution to controlling certain insect pests as both the adult beetles and their larvae are predacious and feed voraciously on mites, aphids and other small insects. Their value as biological control agents is often underestimated by gardeners as Ladybirds are capable of devouring many times their own body weight in pests each day. A little red and black spotted ladybird beetle (*Rodolia cardinalis*) has been specially imported from Australia to combat the destructive bug Cottony Cushion Scale, also known as the Australian Bug (*Icerya purchasi*).

Ladybirds are members of the Coccinellidae family of beetles and are outstanding biological control agents as they feed on a variety of other small insect pests.

Larvae of ladybirds are, like adult ladybirds, predacious and live off other small insects. Here a ladybird larva is busy eating an aphid on an infested plant.

FACT FILE

- Contrary to popular belief, not all Ladybirds eat aphids and other insects.
- Some members of the Ladybird family feed on leaves of fruit and vegetables. These Ladybirds can often be recognised by their hairy and dull rather than smooth and glossy appearance.

The Spotted Amber Ladybird (*Hippodamia variegata*) was originally introduced from Europe and is renowned for its pest-control potential, as it is predacious to many species of aphid as well as various insect eggs and thrips.

BEETLES • 113

A colourful Lunate Ladybird (*Cheilomenes lunata*) enjoys a meal on an aphid-infested plant.

A ladybird larva explores a plant.

It is a fallacy to believe that all Ladybirds are beneficial as some species such as the Potato Ladybird, Nightshade Ladybird and Curcurbit Ladybird are herbivorous and feed on the leaves of various plants. At first glance they look very much like the predacious Ladybirds. A close examination, however, shows that many herbivorous Ladybirds are generally not as bright and shiny as their predacious relatives as they are sometimes covered with a thin layer of downy hair which makes them duller in appearance.

Eggs of both types can generally be found on the underside of leaves. In the case of the predacious Ladybirds the eggs are usually laid on plants already infested with aphids.

Spotted Amber Ladybirds mate on a plant. Eggs will also be laid on a plant already infested with aphids to ensure that the young larvae will have a supply of food after hatching.

Like all larvae the ladybird larva needs to moult a number of times as it outgrows its old skin. During this process, which can take up to an hour, it is very vulnerable to any predators.

When fully grown a ladybird larva rolls itself into a ball and pupates. Ladybird pupae are extremely small and usually adhere to the underside of leaves.

Within five to ten days, depending on prevailing climatic conditions, the pupa will mature and the adult ladybird will emerge.

Fruit Chafer Beetles
Subfamily Cetoniinae

Close-up of Fruit Chafer Beetle (*Anisorrhina* sp.) showing mouthparts. All beetles have chewing mouthparts.

Most gardeners are familiar with these often beautiful but highly destructive beetles that can frequently be found on rose bushes, ornamentals, fruit trees or on the ground where they eat and burrow into overripe fruit. Commonly known as Fruit or Flower Chafers, they are a group of scarab beetles belonging to the subfamily Cetoniinae.

They have bright, often metallic, patterns in red, yellow, black or white stripes, patches or zigzags. The males of some species also have impressive forward-pointing horns and are favourites of many collectors.

The large, white, slug-like larvae of Fruit and Flower Chafers develop in the ground or in compost heaps.

Fruit chafer beetle (*Dicronorrhina derbyana derbyana*).

Black and yellow Garden Fruit Chafer (*Pachnoda sinuata*).

Male Fruit Chafer Beetle (*Dicronorrhina derbyana derbyana*).

A Zig-zag Fruit Chafer (*Anisorrhina flavomaculata*) sinks its head deeply into a rotting banana.

Zig-zag Fruit Chafer (*Anisorrhina* sp.).

Belted Fruit Chafer (*Pedinorrhina* sp.).

A jewel-like Amethyst Fruit Chafer (*Leucocelis amethystina*).

Fact File

- Fruit Chafer Beetles are serious garden and agricultural pests.
- They are closely related to the Dung Beetles and represent the subfamily Cetoniini of the family Scarabaeidae.

Larva of a fruit chafer. The large slug-like larvae of the Fruit Chafer Beetles develop underground or in compost heaps.

WEEVILS
FAMILY CURCULIONIDAE

There are more than 45 000 species of weevils found throughout the world. They are the largest single family as well as one of the most diverse groups of organisms.

They vary in size from 1 mm up to 60 mm in length and are typically characterised by a long, well-developed rostrum, which in some species is considerably longer than the insect's body. Many species also have elbowed antennae extending from roughly midway on the rostrum. When disturbed they often play dead. If left alone, they become active again within a few minutes.

Although most weevils are regarded as pests due to the damage they inflict on fruit, trees, seeds and stored products, many weevils are host-plant specific as they live on one species of plant only. This makes them excellent bio-control agents. Weevils have been imported into South Africa to combat alien plants such as the water hyacinth (*Eichhornia crassipes*) and many others.

Snout Weevil (Family Curculionidae).

The Weevil has a body length of 13 mm.

Weevil on leaf showing snout and antennae.

Blister Beetles
Family Meloidae

The Family Meloidae comprises a number of species collectively referred to as Blister Beetles due to their ability to exude a toxic substance called cantharadin through their leg joints when threatened or handled. Human contact with cantharadin causes severe blistering of the skin and can even be fatal if ingested. Some species are brightly adorned with red or yellow bands across the elytra to warn off predators.

Adult Blister Beetles feed on flowers and plant material and are capable of doing considerable damage in a garden. No attempt should be made to pick them off by hand as is often recommended for the removal of Fruit and Flower Chafers. Ironically, the larvae of many species of Blister Beetles perform a beneficial task as they control grasshoppers and locusts by parasitising their eggs. Others are parasites in the nests of various bees where they live off the nectar and pollen stored in the nest.

Above: CMR Blister Beetles (*Mylabris oculata*) feed on a Cape Honeysuckle. These beetles often occur in large numbers and are capable of rapidly stripping a plant.

Right: Two Blister Beetles fight for territory on a Cape Honeysuckle bush.

Fact File

- Blister Beetles are members of the Meloidae family and can rapidly strip a plant of its blooms. On the positive side, their larvae help control grasshoppers as they are parasites of their eggs.
- Touching a Blister Beetle can cause the skin to blister as it exudes a caustic chemical called cantharadin. This chemical also makes them highly unpalatable to predators.

Darkling Beetles
Family Tenebrionidae

The Family Tenebrionidae to which the Darkling Beetles belong, is a large group of beetles with considerable variation in appearance, behaviour and habitat. Members of this family are found in grassland, bushveld and even harsh desert areas such as the Namib Desert. Certain species are known by the common name of "Toktokkies" due to their habit of using the back end of the abdomen to tap on the ground to attract mates.

1: The Tapering Darkling Beetle (*Himatismus villosus*) has a body length of 14 mm.

2: Darkling beetle (possibly *Psorodes tuberculata*). Note the two sharp spines on the femora (upper part) of the forelegs, which is characteristic of this species.

3: Darkling Beetle (Toktokkie) (Family Tenebrionidae).

Hairy Darkling Beetle (*Lagria vulnerata*). This plant-eating beetle can be a pest on beans.

Predacious Water Beetles
Family Dytiscidae

The bodies of these smooth, oval-shaped, shiny beetles are highly streamlined to allow them to move rapidly through water with the minimum of drag. Their hind legs, which they use as oars, are strongly developed with the last segment flattened and fringed with stiff hairs.

Water Beetles are normally found in still waters including ponds, lakes and river pools. They can remain underwater for extended periods of time by breathing air stored beneath their elytra. Both larvae and adult beetles are voracious predators, feeding on other insects, tadpoles and even small fish. In some species the adult beetles release a powerful defensive chemical capable of stunning nearby fish. Adults are also strong fliers and often fly great distances at night searching for water.

A Yellow-edge Water Beetle (*Cybister tripunctatus*) leaves a wake behind it as it moves rapidly through the water with oar-like legs extended. Body length 30 mm.

Predacious Water Beetles (*Cybister tripunctatus*) trap a reserve of air under their elytra (wing cases) which they are able to draw upon when immersed. This allows them to dive down deeply and remain underwater while hunting prey.

Net-winged Beetles
Family Lycidae

Net-winged Beetles are flattened and pear or leaf-shaped in form as the elytra is much wider toward the rear than at the front. While some species are slim in shape there are others that appear almost squat. Another species has hooks to the front part of the wings. Their name is derived from the delicate network of veins and ridges found on the elytra.

Net-winged Beetles vary in size from 6–22 mm in length and can often found on flowers and foliage or in open areas clinging onto a grass stem. They are fast flyers and will buzz their way from one bush to the next with a flash of orange from their wings. Overall they are red, yellow or orange with black markings or a black band at

A Net-winged Beetle (*Lycus* sp.) with leather-like elytra opened and membranous flying wings extended, about to lift off from a plant.

A Net-winged Beetle (*Lycus* sp.) clearly showing its orange and black colouration as well as the series of veins and ridges on the elytra from which it derives its name.

The Hooked-winged Net-winged Beetle (*Lycus melanurus*). Note the prominent "hooks" on the front part of the forewings.

the back end of the elytra. These strong contrasting colours also serve to warn predators that they are distasteful.

To the casual eye they may appear more like a flying bug than a beetle as they do not have the hardened elytra that most beetles do, their forewings being leather-like rather than hard.

Fact File

Most Ground Beetles rapidly pursue their prey (other insects) at night. A few eat pollen, berries and seeds. The larvae of Ground Beetles are also predators.

Ground Beetles
Family Carabidae

Almost all Ground Beetles are predacious and many have strong, well-developed mouthparts with which they can inflict a vicious bite if handled. The greater part of this family are relentless hunters with the ability to move extremely rapidly over the ground feeding on nearly anything that they can capture.

Ground beetles cannot fly as in many cases their wing cases have been fused together to form a strong protective shell and the membranous hindwings normally used for flying have consequently disappeared.

Some species of Carabidae are best known for their ability to defend themselves by squirting a strong stream of formic acid or other chemicals which can result in serious skin burns or eye injuries.

In size, different species of this family vary from 3 mm to almost 60 mm and some can live for up to four years.

Ground Beetles (shown here possibly *Thermophilum fornasinii*) are swift, ruthless hunters that will make a meal of almost anything that moves. Many Ground Beetles have completely lost the ability to fly but this is well compensated for by the speed with which they can move over the ground.

Fact File

- Over 1 000 beetle species are known to live as predators, parasites or commensals in the nests of ants. They gain entrance to the nest by mimicking the odour and behaviour of the ants.
- The smallest beetle (*Nanosella fungi*) at 0,25 mm in length is some 16 million times smaller in volume than the largest beetle (*Goliathus giganteus*) which may have a body length up to 100 mm.
- Bombardier Beetles, *Brachinus* spp. (Family Carabidae), have the ability to discharge a defensive spray of hot quinones. Two chemical reactants are stored in adjacent compartments of an abdominal gland and combine explosively when the insect is disturbed.

The vicious mandibles of the Ground Beetle can deliver a nasty bite.

The Gregarious Antlion (*Hagenomyia tristis*) is a beautiful and delicate creature with iridescent green eyes and blue tinted wings.

LACEWINGS AND ANTLIONS
ORDER NEUROPTERA

Neuroptera means "nerve wings" and refers to the finely veined and branched wings of these insects.

It is ironic that although nearly all adult Neuroptera are best known for the beauty of their wings, most are rather weak fliers. They are pretty insects with two pairs of large, thin, membranous wings which are extensively and finely veined. In some species these veins create the impression of a finely woven net, while others have wings that are decorated in dotted, speckled or blotched patterns usually in black or shades of grey.

Neuroptera are represented in the country by about 380 species. Members of this family vary greatly in size. The wingspan of some may be as small as 4 mm while others have a wingspan of over 100 mm. Adult Neuroptera generally feed on pollen and nectar although some species, such as the mantidflies, eat other insects. In stark contrast to the delicate beauty of the adults almost all the larvae of this order are voracious feeders and quite vicious looking predators. They feed on a range of other small insects such as aphids and ants.

Lacewings
Family Chrysopidae

Adult Green Lacewings with their small, bright, yellow eyes are sometimes also called Golden-eyed Flies. They are little fragile insects with a wingspan of only about 25 mm. Although their bodies are green, their wings are translucent and covered with a fine lacework of veins, hence their name. They have a pair of long antennae which can even exceed the total body length including that of the wings.

The adults fly by night and are strongly attracted to light. Numerous Lacewings are invariably found congregating around any outdoor light, although they are not often noticed due to their diminutive size. They normally rest with their wings folded roof-like over their abdomens and their antennae extended.

The larvae, on the other hand, are also active by day and can be found on the underside of leaves, especially those of aphid-infested plants. They are insatiable eaters of aphids and other small bugs such as mealy bugs and scale insects as well as mites. This makes them beneficial as predators of agricultural pests. They have been successfully used in the past in biological control programmes to help control the populations of certain pest insects.

A Green Lacewing (*Chrysoperla* sp.) with finely veined wings and long antennae. Body length 13 mm (including wings).

The larvae are equipped with a set of sickle-shaped pincers called mandibles which they use to both pierce their prey as well as to suck their juices out. The larvae of some species have the unusual habit of camouflaging themselves by sticking the skins of their prey on their backs together with an assortment of small twigs and other vegetation. Moving around like this they appear very much like walking junkyards.

Lacewings lay their eggs on thin rigid stalks which are attached to tree trunks or branches, each stalk having a single egg at its tip. The stalks are made from a fluid which they secrete and which then quickly hardens.

Grey Lacewing (possibly *Chrysemosa* sp.).

A Lacewing larva: a voracious eater of aphids and other small insects.

Moth Lacewings (Family Psychopsidae) are rather rare insects.

A Lacewing larva with assorted debris stuck to its back as camouflage.

Antlions
Family Myrmeleontidae

Like the Lacewings, the larvae of Antlions also have specialised mouthparts with large, sickle-shaped mandibles that form pincers. The prey's body juices are sucked out through hollow channels running between the adjacent surfaces of the mouthparts called the mandibles and the maxillae. Unlike the lacewings, however, Antlions are not found on leaves but on or in the ground. Some species are free living and move about just under the surface of loose sand while others construct sandpit traps to capture their prey.

The pit sand trap of an Antlion larva. Any unsuspecting insect venturing close to its rim will find itself sliding down the smooth sides into the clutches of the waiting Antlion.

An Antlion larva with mandibles just protruding above the sand waits for its prey.

The sandpit traps of Antlions are common throughout South Africa and are found wherever there is soft, loose sand. They are easily identified by the snake-like trails that can often be seen leading to them early in the morning as the Antlion larvae normally move about by night. These trails are formed by the Antlions' strange rearwards shuffle as these insects always move backward.

Readers who have grown up in country areas are no doubt familiar with the round sandpit traps of the Antlion with their sloping sides. Children often delight in sticking a thin stalk or blade of grass into the trap which usually results in the Antlion pouncing on it and hanging on tenaciously while it is pulled from its hole. If the insect is then placed back on the ground, a short distance from its hole, it will rapidly shuffle backwards. When it has found a suitable spot it starts digging its way into the sand.

It first creates a small circle in the sand and then, as it digs downwards, it shoots particles of sand out of the hole with a flick of its head. As it progresses, the sides become steeper and lined with loose sand creating a perfect funnel shape. The Antlion now settles down at the bottom where it lies in wait for its dinner. It may lie completely covered just under

An Antlion larva. These strange looking little creatures move backward with shuffle-like movements.

The sickle-shaped jaws of the Antlion are able to pierce its prey and then suck out the body contents.

A magnificently patterned adult Antlion.

the surface or it may have its open pincers projecting above the surface in readiness. Any hapless insect that now approaches the edge of the pit will find itself sliding down the sides of loose sand right into the grip of the Antlion.

Antlion larvae do not feed only on ants, as their name implies, but capture almost anything that they can subdue, sometimes even insects much larger than themselves.

Adult Antlion with wings spread.

An adult Veld Antlion (*Palpares* sp.) with fine lace-like wings.

LACEWINGS AND ANTLIONS • 131

In contrast to its small, rather grotesque larvae measuring only a few millimetres in length, adult Antlions are relatively large, gracious and delicate insects, some with wingspans of more than 100 mm. They superficially resemble dragonflies or damselflies in general appearance and are often seen as such by the casual observer. A closer examination, however, reveals that Antlions have longer, more prominent antennae which end in a club shape, whereas dragonflies have short thin antennae. Furthermore, where the dragonfly is an excellent flier, Antlions are slow and clumsy in flight. They are also active by night while dragonflies fly only by day.

The large and colourful wings of several species of Antlions are indeed some of the most exquisite found on

Gregarious Antlions (*Hagenomyia tristis*) group together under the heavy shade of a tree.

An adult Antlion (*Palpares* sp.) seen close up showing its heavy antennae and chewing mouthparts.

any insect. On inspection they are seen to have a network of finely laced veins on a membranous background of yellow, green, blue, grey or even a combination of some or all of these colours. Superimposed on this are bold solid or broken lines in stark black, or blotches, flecks and speckles of black, grey or blue.

MANTIDFLIES
FAMILY MANTISPIDAE

These are strange little insects which, when seen for the first time, seem to be some sort of bizarre cross between a praying mantid and a lacewing. The Mantidfly has what appears to be the body and wings complete with an intricate network of veins of the lacewing, while it has a neck and head similar to that of a mantid. To add to this odd picture it also has raptorial forelegs which, like the mantid, it keeps raised in front of its head and uses to capture other insects. Some species are also good wasp mimics and have adopted the brown and yellow colouration of some paper wasps.

The larvae of the Mantidfly feed on spider eggs and also parasitise spiders' egg sacs in which they pupate.

> **FACT FILE**
> - The larval lifespan of Antlion larvae can be as long as three years while adults live for approximately a month.
> - Lacewing and Antlion larvae have incomplete digestive systems in which the anus is sealed. Waste materials accumulate in the gut and are only expelled after pupation in the form of a pellet known as a meconium.

The unusual and carnivorous little Mantidfly (Family Mantispidae). Like a mantid it has long raptorial forelegs. Body size 18 mm.

Recently hatched nymphs of the common garden locust.

Grasshoppers and Crickets
Order Orthoptera

The name "Orthoptera" is formed from the Greek words "ortho" and "ptera" meaning "straight wing". This refers to the parallel-sided structure of the front wings of these insects.

Grasshoppers, crickets, locusts and katydids all fall into the Order Orthoptera of which there are more than 20 000 species worldwide. Many of them vary considerably in general appearance and are found in a variety of habitats. Some live on plants and others on the ground. Certain species of crickets live in deep burrows underground while there are also wingless species that live in caves. They also inhabit a wide range of biomes from dry sandy areas to wet soggy ground to bushveld and savanna.

Whereas grasshoppers and locusts have short and in some species even stubby or sword-like antennae, the somewhat similar-looking katydids as well as the crickets have lengthy and thread-like or filiform antennae which in most cases are much longer than their body length. In some species they can be as much as five times the body length.

Order Orthoptera is split into two distinct suborders to accommodate these differences. The Enseferia or long-horned species contain all the families that have antennae consisting of more than 30 segments or joints (annuli) and the Caelifera or short-horned grasshoppers contain the remaining members of the order.

Katydids and crickets are thus placed in the subfamily Enseferia (long-horned) while all the grasshoppers and locusts belong to the subfamily Caelifera (short-horned grasshoppers).

Despite the order name clearly referring to wings, some members of this order such as certain species of mole crickets and cave crickets, have no wings at all, while others have reduced wings or only small stubby forewings. Most, however, are characterised by having two pairs of wings, of which the hindwings or flying wings fold in like a folding fan under the forewings.

The hindwings are delicate and membranous but large in comparison to the forewings. In some species of grasshoppers and locusts they are brightly coloured in contrasting shades, often of red and black. When in danger, these wings are opened up and displayed in a threatening manner to ward off an aggressor. The forewings, called tegmina, are tough and leathery and serve to protect the flying wings.

While some species of grasshoppers are strong fliers, grasshoppers and crickets are better known for their jumping ability. Many can jump great lengths in comparison to their body size. This is achieved by long, strong hindlegs that have broad, heavily developed muscular upper parts (femora) designed to extend the legs quickly and with great force. The hindlegs of katydids, on the other hand, appear to be rather long and slender when compared to those of the grasshoppers and crickets. They are still adept jumpers and do so without hesitation if threatened. However, they prefer moving slowly about on vegetation rather than jumping and there is at least one species of katydid (*Megalotheca longiceps*) which is unable to fly.

Most Orthoptera are herbivorous and feed on a variety of vegetation. Some are omnivorous while others such as certain katydids and crickets are carnivorous and feed on other insects. A few even deliver a nasty bite if picked up.

A Common Stick Grasshopper (*Acrida acuminata*) well camouflaged against a background of vegetation.

A "Rooibaadjie" also known as a Koppie Foam Grasshopper.

GRASSHOPPERS AND CRICKETS • 135

A pair of Elegant Grasshoppers (*Zonocerus elegans*), their striking colours highlighted by late afternoon sunshine, mate on a grass stalk.

Many of the grasshoppers and katydids are coloured to blend in with grasses or other vegetation. Some grasshoppers so closely resemble grass stems in form and colouration that they are virtually impossible to detect in the veld unless they move. Other grasshoppers and crickets are stone or granite coloured to blend in with the ground.

In contrast to this, one family of grasshoppers, the Pyrgomorphidae, are conspicuously brightly coloured in striking contrasting colours of black, red and green. Locally they sport noteworthy names such as Rooibaadjie and Elegant Grasshopper.

The Orthoptera is probably one of the most destructive groups of plant-feeding insects. Some species, such as the Brown Locust (*Locustana pardalina*), move in great swarms of millions of individuals, devouring any greenery in their path. They can cut a swathe through large tracts of land and totally decimate any crops. This behaviour takes place periodically and appears to be linked to the population density at any given time. When the density becomes too great within a certain area, they are stimulated to swarm. This propensity to swarm is limited to a few species of grasshoppers and also differentiates the locusts from the grasshoppers as those grasshoppers that swarm are called locusts. Swarming locusts present a considerable problem in South Africa's arid Karoo regions where recurring outbreaks take place.

Locust swarms offer a feast for scores of reptiles and birds that gorge themselves on the young locusts. Many bird species such as kestrels, starlings and storks to mention just a few are attracted by these swarms. Although this does away with great numbers of locusts and the presence of these birds needs to be encouraged, chemical means are usually used to exterminate the swarms or to control the locust population before they reach swarm density. In spite of the fact that the chemicals used today are considerably more environmentally friendly than those used in past years, they do still kill a great number of other insects including the essential pollinators that are the lifeblood of the Karoo veld.

Stridulations, the chirping or rasping songs produced by many of the Orthoptera, play an important part in the courtship and mating behaviour of most species. Depending on the particular family, these sounds are produced either by rubbing the upper surface of one forewing against the lower surface of the other, the wings being equipped with scrapers and file-like veins for this purpose, or by rubbing the hindleg against the forewing. Some species apparently

An Elegant Grasshopper clings to a grass stalk.

also produce ultrasonic sounds which cannot be heard by the human ear.

Crickets are especially prolific sound producers. Serenading males can be accurately located over great distances by a receptive female. The song of each individual species also has its own distinctive quality and attracts only members of that particular species. Mole Crickets produce a low buzzing sound and use their burrows to further amplify their stridulations. The Tree Cricket has the loudest call of all as it ingeniously uses a hole that it has chewed in a leaf to act as a baffle to amplify its song. The frequency of stridulations of these insects is also influenced by the prevailing temperature. The air temperature in degrees centigrade can be calculated by adding 11 to the number of chirps a tree cricket (*Oecanthus capensis*) makes in three seconds.

Of all insects the Tree Crickets are possibly the most frustrating to locate in the bush. Although their call can be clearly heard when at a distance, the moment they sense the slightest movement they change the position of their baffle by swinging their bodies or wings in relation to the leaf through which they are calling. This has the perceived effect of changing the direction of the sound. One moment the creature appears to be calling from right next to you, the next it seems far off and in quite another direction.

As a matter of general interest, I have found a method of reasonably accurately determining the position of most stridulating crickets except the Tree Crickets which still regularly manage to elude me. I use a vuvuzella, the loud horn-like instrument so popular at soccer matches and these days obtainable at most supermarkets. By holding this up against my ear in the same way that an ear-horn is used and slowly swinging it from left to right while carefully listening to the change in volume of the sound, the insect's position can be quite accurately pinpointed.

The tympanic organs or ears of crickets and katydids resemble the surface or skin of a drum. They are situated on their fore tibia or front legs and appear as small oblong discs that can be easily identified with the use of a low-power magnifying glass. The tympanic organs of grasshoppers are found on the sides of the abdomen on the first segment.

No chapter on the Orthoptera would be complete without at least mentioning the traditional role that crickets have played throughout the centuries in certain cultures. The cricket culture in China, for example, dates back some 2 000 years where the cricket was believed to be the bringer of happiness and good fortune. Throughout the centuries the Chinese have built special and elaborate little cricket cages for keeping singing crickets captive. These cages were often constructed from wood, brass, bone and even gold and were hung in homes so that the family could enjoy the cricket's song. Even today the collecting, breeding and keeping of singing crickets remains a popular pastime in some of the Eastern cultures.

A burrow-living cricket, the red-headed Nasidius Cricket (*Nasidius* sp.) is of the same family as the notorious Parktown Prawn, although considerably smaller. Note the long, robust ovipositor of this female.

The Common Garden Cricket (*Gryllus bimaculatus*).

As Bei Ju-Yi of the Tang dynasty wrote:

The singing cricket chirps throughout the long night, tolling in the cloudy autumn with its rain. Intent on disturbing the gloomy sleepless soul, the cricket moves towards the bed chirp by chirp.

And from John Keats the following extract from *On the Grasshopper and the Cricket*:

... The poetry of earth is ceasing never
On a lone winter evening, when the frost
Has wrought a silence, from the stove there shrills
The Cricket's song, in warmth increasing ever; ...

Fact File

- Many species of Orthoptera use their song to attract a mate. However, when they detect a competing male in their territory they produce different sound signals to drive it away.
- Each species produces a unique mating call. Mating calls are often used by entomologists to distinguish between species.

Short-horned Grasshoppers
Family Acrididae

This is by far the largest of the grasshopper families with about 356 species found in southern Africa. It encompasses all the commonly seen grasshoppers and swarming locusts and includes damaging species such as the Brown Locust.

In many cases there is not much to visually differentiate many of the species except for small variations in colour and even then several species are similar looking. However, those that do differ in appearance differ quite considerably, such as the Stick Grasshopper with its greatly extended head and horn-like antennae.

Many species of the large family Acrididae are very similar in size and appearance, differing only in colouration.

Fact File

- Most species of grasshoppers deposit their eggs in the ground in small clusters.
- Crickets usually deposit each egg singly in the ground or in tiny splits in the stems of a plant.
- Katydids deposit their eggs in splits made in leaves.

The Garden Locust is a common visitor to suburban gardens throughout South Africa. Note the sharp white and red spines on the hind leg. These are quite capable of inflicting a nasty wound if the insect is handled carelessly and allowed to kick out.

Seen from the back a Stick Grasshopper nymph creates a pattern in harmony with its long hind legs, curved body and sword-like antennae.

A nymph of the Garden Locust. A nymph is green but as it matures will turn brown and develop the characteristic cream stripe along the back by which the adult locust can be identified.

Burrowing Grasshopper (*Acrotylus* sp.). These grasshoppers have long middle legs used for digging and will bury themselves if threatened.

In contrast to the drab appearance of the Burrowing Grasshopper its membranous hindwings are banded in bright orange and black.

The beautiful and striking Stick Grasshopper (*Acrida acuminata*), with its elongated head and prominent eyes, is also a member of the Acrididae family.

WINGLESS GRASSHOPPERS
FAMILY LENTULIDAE

This is a small family with only about 49 species of short-horn grasshoppers. They are all wingless and are also unable to produce any sound. Most are thick and stubby, almost slug-like in appearance.

Paralentula sp., a member of the Lentulidae family of wingless grasshoppers.

FOAM GRASSHOPPERS
FAMILY PYRGOMORPHIDAE

This family of grasshoppers is generally large and slow moving but always conspicuous and brightly coloured. Their striking combinations of contrasting yellow, black, red and green colouration acts as a sign to predators that they are highly distasteful and usually poisonous. Pyrgomorphid grasshoppers are herbivorous and many feed on milkweed (Asclepiadaceae) which is also the source of the powerful toxins stored in their bodies that are capable of killing dogs and even humans if eaten.

In addition to their aposematic body colours, when threatened they may suddenly flash their vividly coloured hindwings as a further warning. Some can also discharge

A magnificent Elegant Grasshopper displays its colours.

Above left: Koppie Foam Grasshopper (*Dictyophorus spumans*). When threatened these grasshoppers give off a poisonous foam derived from the milkweed on which they feed.
Above right: A closer look at the Milkweed Locust.
Left: Another toxic grasshopper, the very common Milkweed Locust (*Phymateus morbillosus*), is found throughout large parts of South Africa.

a foul smelling and nauseating foam from their thorax. These formidable defences allow them to move about their business with almost total impunity from attack by predators, as birds and the like are well aware of the danger they face should they attempt to pick up one of these insects.

In spite of their rather unpleasant attributes, they are overall striking and beautiful creatures. Some display bright red or green serrated knobs on their thorax while others have green and black striped bodies with green or red legs. Their antennae are short but thick and impressive and can vary in colour from a deep black to red or orange.

Long-horned Crickets and Katydids
King Cricket
Family Anostostomatidae

King Crickets are the largest of all crickets and have a body length of 70 mm or more. They are generally not often seen as they are nocturnal and live underground in forest biomes, only coming out to hunt at night. However, one species has found its way into lush suburban gardens in South Africa's Highveld where it now makes recurrent seasonal appearances causing great consternation to residents. Locally named Parktown Prawns, its scientific name is *Libanasidus vittatus*. As they are attracted to light, these huge insects often find their way into homes.

They are strong jumpers and when approached will leap into the air. They also have the rather obnoxious

A King Cricket (*Libanasidus vittatus*), the infamous "Parktown Prawn" has invaded many parts of Johannesburg and Pretoria. It has become notorious for its ability to jump as well as to spray a foul smelling liquid.

The scimitar-shaped ovipositor of the female King Cricket is used for laying eggs.

The powerful hind legs of the King Cricket are well armed with spikes and spurs and have a claw at the end of the foot (tarsus).

A male King Cricket in the entrance to his burrow. Note the absence of an ovipositor.

habit of squirting black, foul-smelling faeces when threatened. Like many Orthoptera they can, if handled, deliver a hefty kick with their spiked hind legs resulting in a nasty scratch or even drawing blood.

In appearance they are reddish in colour with orange legs. The abdomen which is also red/orange is adorned with black bands. The female can easily be recognised by her large scimitar-shaped ovipositor, the organ with which eggs are laid. Male King Crickets develop prominent protruding mandibles or mouthparts which look very much like tusks.

During the day King Crickets hide in their burrows which they have excavated in moist soil by digging with their front legs and throwing back the ground with their hind legs. They are omnivorous and eat both plant and animal material. They are voracious eaters of garden slugs and snails and consequently deliver a valuable and beneficial service to gardeners by controlling the snail population. They also eat rotting plant material and other insects such as cutworms.

The Anostostomatidae family of which the King Cricket is a member, is an old one as shown by fossil evidence of these crickets dating back to the late Triassic period, more than 200 million years ago.

The "monster" from close up – King Crickets are the largest of all crickets.

Top: The palps are sensory appendages of the mouthparts.
Above: The mandibles of a King Cricket.

Mole Cricket
Family Gryllotalpidae

The African Mole Cricket (*Gryllotalpa africana*) is a sturdy and rather hairy, brown-coloured cricket that grows to a length of about 30 mm. It can easily be recognised by its large eyes and overdeveloped, shovel-like forelegs which have been modified for digging.

As its name implies, it lives in deep burrows in the ground where it feeds primarily on roots. Although typically found in wet and marshy areas especially those surrounding dams or rivers, Mole Crickets often establish themselves in well-watered gardens or lawns and can be pests in areas such as golf courses.

A Mole Cricket (*Gryllotalpa africana*). Note the short forewings, which are characteristic of this species. Body length 38 mm.

Grasshoppers and Crickets • 147

Close-up of Mole Cricket showing the head as well as the overdeveloped forelegs, which are used for digging.

An unidentified cricket rests momentarily on the bark of a fallen stump.

The Tree Cricket is also sometimes called a Thermometer Cricket as the prevailing temperature can be measured by its chirps.

Katydids
Family Tettigoniidae

Although katydids in many ways superficially resemble grasshoppers, they are in fact more closely related to crickets. The name katydid comes from an American species that produces a song that sounds very much like "Katy did ... Katy didn't". In South Africa they are commonly called Bush Crickets or simply long-horned grasshoppers because of their long antennae.

Females of some species also have long, sometimes curved, ovipositors. Eggs are laid either in the ground in plant tissue or in leaves which the katydid first splits open before depositing the eggs between the two halves.

Many are green in colour while others are tan, brown or speckled brown. Several are wonderful leaf mimics, having adopted not only the shape and colour of a leaf but also the finest and most astounding patterns of leaf venation. Some katydids can be difficult to spot due to their effective camouflage. Also, many of them are only active at night and either move slowly about foliage or remain sitting quite still during the daylight hours.

They are attracted to light and one may from time to time find a katydid sitting on a lighted window or even entering a home. It is often easiest to track them at

A magnificent True Leaf Katydid (*Zabalius aridus*). Note the blue and bright orange hind legs, the raised orange tubercles on the shield-like pronotum and the "ears" on the front legs just below the "knees".

A Leaf Katydid with a heavy, curved ovipositor feeding on foliage. This is probably a *Phaneroptera* species, which is found throughout the country.

A tiny nocturnal Long-horn Grasshopper (species unidentified) explores a flower.

A True Leaf Katydid (*Zabalius aridus*) closely resembles the foliage on which it is standing.

Eye to eye with a katydid, showing its large chewing mouthparts. The upper lip is termed the labrum, the lower lip the labium. The green structures on the sides are the palps.

Fact File

- The sounds made by Orthoptera are produced by stridulation.
- Long-horned species rub the upper surface of one wing against the lower surface of another wing.
- Short-horned species rub the inner surface of the hind leg against the outer surface of the front wing.

night by following their song which they produce by rubbing the sharp edge of a front wing, known as a scraper, against the rough edge or file on the bottom of the other front wing. Their wings also have a small circular membranous area near the wing bases called a mirror which amplifies the sound.

An interesting experiment with katydids, or in fact any stridulating cricket, is to record the sound with a tape recorder and then play it back at a slower speed. If the play-back speed is slow enough, each individual chirp that makes up the song can be heard. The fullness and clarity of each note produced by some of these insects is unbelievable when listened to in this way.

The "ears" or tympanal organs of katydids are located on their front legs, just below their "knees". On some species these can easily be seen while in others they are not quite so obvious. The female can follow the mating call of the male by orientating her "ears" in the appropriate direction.

Katydids are mostly vegetarian and, depending on the species, feed on plants, grasses, seeds, leaves and fruit while some also eat small insects, insect eggs and larvae. There are also carnivorous species which prey on larger insects and some of these can inflict a nasty bite if carelessly handled.

Violet Dropwing dragonfly (*Trithemis annulata*) in resting position with wings dropped forwards and downwards.

Dragonflies and Damselflies
Order Odonata

The name Odonata comes from the Greek "odonto-" meaning tooth and refers to the strong teeth found on the mandibles of most adults.

Dragonflies are generally thought to be among the first insects to have taken to the air with fossil evidence suggesting they date back about 300 million years. Early relatives of the modern dragonfly, the griffenflies, also included the largest known insect with a wingspan of 640 mm (*Meganeuropsis permiana*).

Today, Odonata is divided into two distinct suborders, the Anisoptera or dragonflies and the Zygoptera, better known as damselflies.

Both dragonflies and damselflies have powerful biting mouthparts with strongly toothed mandibles, from which the order gets its name. They are also both terrestrial and free living in their adult stages but their nymphs, known as naiads, are aquatic. They live underwater and feed on other aquatic insects, tadpoles and even small fish. These naiads in turn form part of the diets of other aquatic predators such as fish.

Naiads have unusual mouthparts that are found only among the Odonata. The lower lip or labium is extended into a long organ called a mask which is kept folded against the lower part of the head. At the tip of the mask is a pair of pincers used for capturing prey. When a suitable candidate approaches the naiad, it shoots out this mask, captures the prey with its pincers and then brings its victim to its mouth.

Depending on the particular species, the dragonfly naiad lives in its aquatic environment for anything from a month to about three years. When mature, it makes its way out of the water and onto a stick, weed or trunk of a nearby tree onto which it can cling. Here an astounding transformation takes place. The hard chitinous outer skin of the naiad splits and a fully developed dragonfly emerges. After emergence, the dragonfly remains stationary, clinging either to the old skin or to the plant while its own skin dries and its wings expand, stiffen and harden. Suddenly, it launches itself into the air, leaving behind the dry translucent shell of the naiad.

Odonata have a unique way of mating. Before mating takes place the male deposits a packet of sperm into a special receptacle on the second segment of his abdomen, just behind the thorax. Using claspers at the end of his abdomen, he then locks onto a female, holding her firmly just behind the head. She, in turn, bends her abdomen forwards and upwards under her body and removes the sperm from the male's receptacle. This rather convoluted mating position is called a wheel.

Right: A naiad, the voracious aquatic nymph of a dragonfly.
Below: A fierce hunter, the powerful, toothed mouthparts of the dragonfly allow it to quickly deal with any prey.

The dried out skin of a dragonfly naiad hangs from the branch of a tree.

Dragonflies may mate on the wing flying in tandem in the wheel position or settle on a suitable perch. Damselflies generally mate in a stationary position while clinging to a grass stalk, twig or stem. The mating organs of Odonata are often species specific and operate on a lock and key principle.

A male can only mate with a female of the same species as the lock and key of both need to match. Microscopic studies of the abdominal appendages or claspers of male damselflies together with their unique construction are often the only way to identify many of the diverse species.

While female dragonflies deposit their eggs directly into water by flying over the surface and dipping their ovipositors into the water, damselflies generally lay their eggs in holes pierced in reeds or stems of other water plants.

Odonata require good oxygen levels and unpolluted water to survive and breed. Many of the more common species are found throughout the country wherever there is suitable water or wetlands. Others are endemic to certain habitats. They are also important bio-indicators of water quality. Although many are moderately tolerant, some species especially those of the damselflies, such as members of the Calopterygidae, Chlorocyphidae and Platycnemidae families, have low to very low tolerance to pollution.

Dragonflies

Dragonflies are large, active, swift-flying, carnivorous insects. They have two pairs of broad wings which vary in size, the hindwings being larger than the forewings. The wings also widen to a broad base and are held spread open or with certain species known as dropwings, dropped downwards and forwards when at rest. The wings of both dragonflies and damselflies have complex patterns of veins which strengthen and support the wings and which are often essential factors in differentiating between various species.

Dragonflies are exceptionally strong and agile fliers and are said to reach speeds of 60 km/h. They capture their prey in flight using their specially adapted legs which are set well forward. The legs form an oval-shaped basket with which they scoop other insects out of the air. The legs are also densely covered with bristles that facilitate the capture and holding of their prey. Although efficient for capturing prey, this unusual placement of their legs, with the feet almost in line with the front of the head, is of little use for walking. Dragonflies are thus limited to using their legs to cling onto vegetation or reeds when at rest.

Julia Skimmer dragonflies mating. This pair first spent some time flying in tandem in the "wheel" position before settling on a water plant stem.

Julia Skimmer dragonfly (*Orthetrum julia*). This species rests with its wings held downwards.

A scarlet dragonfly, possibly a Wandering Glider, settles on a leaf.

Red-veined Dropwing dragonfly (*Trithemis arteriosa*).

A dragonfly explores a muddy pool after a thunderstorm.

To add to their prowess as hunters, they have mobile heads and exceptional eyesight. The large compound eyes cover most of the head and virtually meet at the top of the head allowing them to see to the top, bottom and sides. In some species each eye contains up to 28 000 individual facets.

> ### Fact File
> Most dragonfly naiads move forward by "jet propulsion". Rapid contraction of the rectal muscles forces water out the rear end and shoots the insect forward.

Violet Dropwing (*Trithemis annulata*).

Damselflies

Even though dragonflies and damselflies have much in common there is also a number of distinct features that differentiate them.

In contrast to the dragonflies, the wings of damselflies are of even size and are narrow at the base where they join the thorax. When at rest most species of damselflies hold their wings closed over the back.

Damselflies are smaller and considerably more delicate than dragonflies. They are also not such proficient fliers and prefer to remain sitting on vegetation in shady spots, from time to time darting out to capture a small insect.

Their eyes are significantly smaller than those of dragonflies. They are widely separated and never meet at the top of the head as the eyes of dragonflies do. There are many more damselfly species than dragonflies.

> ### Fact File
> - Many adult male dragonflies establish and defend territories along the perimeter of a lake or stream.
> - Females only mate with males that hold a territory so population density is regulated by territory size.

Bluetail Damselflies (*Ischnura* sp.) mate while clinging to a grass stem. Note how the male (above) holds the female with his claspers while she lifts her abdomen up and under to collect sperm from his sperm receptacle.

Damselflies are beautiful and delicate insects that belong to the suborder Zygoptera. They are considerably smaller than the more robust dragonflies with which they share the order Odonata. They are generally difficult to identify in the field as colour, size and markings can vary between sexes and even amongst members of the same sex and species. Careful examination of wing venation, markings and abdominal appendages under magnification are the only ways of positively identifying many species.

Fact File

Male damselflies have a special flagellum that can reach into a female's body and remove sperm deposited by another male in a previous mating.

Head of an adult cockroach showing mouthparts.

Cockroaches
Order Blattodea

The name Blattodea comes from "blatta", the Greek word for cockroach.

The one insect order that everyone has to deal with at some stage or another is the cockroaches and of all insects, they are also possibly the most despised. A little known fact among householders who generally have to deal with the American, German or Oriental Cockroaches that periodically find their way into kitchens and pantries, is that there are some 4 000 different species of cockroaches worldwide with about 175 species in southern Africa. Of these, only about 1% are pests and only a small number of species ever enter the average home. Most cockroaches are nocturnal and live outdoors under leaf litter, rocks, bark, fallen trees or on vegetation. Many are restricted to certain regions such as the Cape Zebra Cockroach and Table Mountain Cockroach which are endemic to parts of the Western Cape.

Cockroaches are ancient insects and capable survivors as attested to by the longevity of the group and their great diversity. Fossil evidence dates them to about 320 million years ago, to the Late Carboniferous period. During their long existence they have changed very little which indicates their success as a group. Individuals of species such as the American Cockroach can live up to 4 years.

Cockroaches are closely related to grasshoppers and crickets (Orthoptera) as well as mantids (Mantodea) and at one stage were classified as a family of the Order Orthoptera. Today they are accommodated in the Order Blattodea.

Blattodea play an important ecological role. As general feeders and scavengers, they help decompose forest litter, animal matter and other waste. They have chewing mouthparts with toothed mandibles and can digest a wide range of matter. Their digestive systems contain a variety of bacteria and protozoa which help break down various substances.

Due to their generalised morphology, cockroaches, especially the large American Cockroach (*Periplaneta americana*), are often used in laboratories as subjects for experimentation and studies of insect biology. In some parts of the world, cockroaches are even kept as pets, for example the large, flightless Madagascan Hissing Cockroach (*Gromphadorhina portentosa*) which can hiss loudly by forcing air through its spiracles. In South Africa avid anglers sometimes breed American Cockroaches as fish bait in cages fitted with flat sheets of wood stacked about 1 cm apart between which the cockroaches hide and breed.

Although usually associated with dirty and unhygienic conditions, the cockroach is itself a clean insect which spends much time cleaning itself. Their tendency to scavenge in places such as sewers, drains and refuse from where they can convey contaminated material into dwellings makes them a health risk. Additionally, many species may carry bacteria such as Salmonella in their gut which they can pass on through their saliva and faeces.

Cockroaches breed prolifically. With some species eggs are enclosed in a hardened sheath or case known as an ootheca which the female carries around with her for

Many of the wild cockroaches such as this one live outdoors amongst leaf litter where they feed on rotting vegetation.

An adult male and female American Cockroach. The male appears large as it has longer wings.

a few days before dropping it. Others retract the ootheca into a brood pouch where the eggs develop inside the body of the female and the young nymphs are born alive. A typical ootheca of the American Cockroach contains 14 to 16 eggs but can contain many more.

American Cockroach (*Periplaneta americana*) adult female and two nymphs at different stages of development. Only mature adults have wings.

Although there are insects such as various groups of wasps which parasitise cockroach ootheca, when dropped indoors in cavities or cracks they are virtually indestructible. This is why householders trying to exterminate cockroaches need to follow up treatment of the infested areas from time to time as the eggs hatch. The nymphs emerge from the egg case in about six to eight weeks and mature in about six to twelve months depending on factors such as temperature and available food sources.

After hatching, the nymphs are tiny and white, almost transparent, in colour. Over a period of several hours, they slowly darken to a uniform brown colour. Growth takes place fairly slowly and the nymphs moult a number of times before attaining adulthood. The nymphs are white after moulting and take about two or three hours to darken. One often hears of someone reporting having seen an albino cockroach – these are undoubtedly nymphs that have recently moulted.

Not all cockroaches have wings. Those that do only develop wings once they are fully mature. Although winged species can fly, they seldom seem to do so. Most are fast runners and prefer moving about in this manner.

I can personally attest to the speed with which these creatures can move. I recently had occasion to accept an assignment to photograph cockroaches for use on packaging for a cockroach insecticide. I managed to obtain from an angler who breeds them, a number of specimens of American Cockroaches consisting of an assortment of large winged adults and a selection of nymphs of various ages. I placed these into a glass tank to observe and photograph as necessary. While attempting to isolate a particular female with attached ootheca, I inadvertently knocked the lid off the tank. In a second a number of large winged individuals managed to escape and scuttle from my workbench onto the floor and behind various racks and shelves. As my laboratory/studio, which is a spare room in the house, usually contains an assortment of living insects in various stages of development, it was not an option to use any sort of spray insecticide. Each one of the escaped cockroaches thus had to be found and captured individually by hand, a task which took most of the morning and caused a great deal of consternation. I am pleased to say, however, that my wife is again talking to me.

The egg cases or ootheca of the American Cockroach.

The Oriental Cockroach (*Blatta orientalis*).

An outdoor "wild" cockroach, possibly *Oxyhaloa* sp.

An adult American Cockroach (*Periplaneta americana*).

Harvester Termite workers cut grass which they carry into their nests. These termites can severely damage lawns as well as grazing land.

TERMITES
ORDER ISOPTERA

The name Isoptera is derived from the Greek "iso" meaning equal and "ptera" meaning wings and refers to the similar shape and size of the wings.

The insects commonly called "white ants", "flying ants" or in Afrikaans, "rysmiere", are not ants at all, but termites. In fact, they are not even closely related to ants but rather show a close relationship to cockroaches. A cursory study of a termite shows that it does not have a segmented waist as ants do. It is also a fatter, softer, shorter-legged and generally much slower moving insect. However, like the Hymenoptera which are the ants, bees and wasps, termites also build and live in large communal nests. They are the only other insects apart from the Hymenoptera to have a complex social structure in their nests.

Termites are highly social insects and their nests can contain from several hundred to several million individuals with each a member of a specific caste, performing specific duties in the nest to the benefit of all. This cooperation between individuals, guided by an instinct known as swarm intelligence, allows them to make the most of available food sources and exploit environments that would not be accessible to any single insect alone. A typical colony contains nymphs, workers, soldiers, fertile individuals of both sexes as well as larger male reproductives called kings and one or more huge and ungainly egg-laying queens.

The primary task of the kings and queens is to breed and a queen can lay several thousand eggs a day. Unlike ant societies where the queen mates only once and then stores the male's sperm for life, a termite king continues to mate with the queen.

The worker caste is by far the largest and contains the most individuals in a termite nest. Workers do all the routine tasks required to support the colony and maintain the nest such as building and repairs. They also forage for food and feed the other castes and the nymphs. Termites do not have a larval stage as ants do. In some species the workers have no eyes and are thus blind, while in others such as the Harvester Termites, eyes are present.

The soldiers defend the nest and protect the colony from potential enemies, especially ants as a number of species prey on termites or their eggs. Termite soldiers have large heads and well-developed mandibles. The mandibles are sometimes so large that the soldiers are unable to feed themselves and need to rely on workers to feed them. In many species the soldiers are also blind.

Termites are generally known for the enormous towering mud mounds that they construct. Mounds are built from a cement-like mixture of fine sand and saliva. These mounds are so sturdily constructed that they are known to be capable of damaging industrial machinery. In a long established colony living under favourable environmental conditions, a mound can exceed 4 m in height.

A single worker drags a large blade of grass into the nest.

A termite infected with mites. These tiny mites appear to be quite at home scuttling around on the termite.

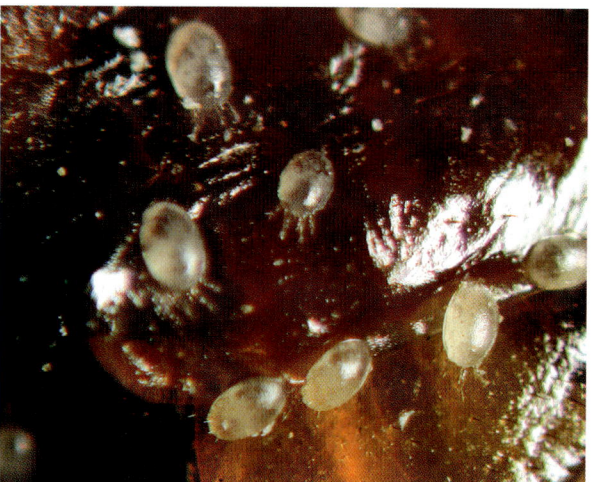

A closer look at the mites. Their exact function or relationship with the termite is unknown.

A soldier, worker and nymph of the Northern Harvester Termite (*Hodotermes mossambicus*).

Termite mounds are not just random piles of mud but are constructed with systems of complex ducts and channels to ventilate, regulate and control the internal environments of the nest which may be a metre or more below the ground. Not all termites construct these towers. Some species build only low mounds while others do not build mounds above ground at all.

There are more than 2 300 species of known termites worldwide. Most typically feed on dead plant material such as wood, dead grass and dry animal dung while certain species also cultivate and feed on fungus. Some species enclose their food source in a covering of plaster before proceeding to break it down. They can digest woody fibres with the help of bacteria that live in their stomachs.

Often a dead tree trunk is encountered in the veld with a portion or even the whole of it plastered over with clay. If you should encounter one of these on which termites are active and you break away a small opening in the cement, you will find soldiers rapidly rallying to the opening to defend the breach while workers scuttle about to repair it.

Termites are important decomposers that help to break down dead wood and other vegetation and return the plant nutrients to the soil. Their wood-feeding habits, however, can cause them to become significant pests in both urban and rural areas as they will attack any untreated wood used for building and other commercial products. In the more arid parts of South Africa, Harvester Termites are also serious commercial pests of grazing land as they remove the grass cover which is often sparse, and thus compete with stock and game animals for limited grazing.

The fierce toothed mandibles of a soldier. The soldiers of many species are blind but the Northern Harvester Termite (*Hodotermes mossambicus*) has eyes.

Termite nymphs at various stages of development.

A termite mound of almost 2 metres high. These mounds are natural marvels of engineering and assist to control the temperature inside the nest.

The entrance to a disused termite nest. Termite nests and mounds are often utilised by different animals for nesting.

A dead termite is dragged away by one of its arch-enemies, an ant. Many species of ant regularly raid termite nests.

Fact File

- The word "termite" comes from a Latin word, meaning "wood worm".
- Some termite soldiers can spray noxious liquids through either a horn-like nozzle called a nasus or an opening in the front of the head known as a fontanelle.
- Termites have symbiotic bacteria and protozoans in their guts that help them digest tough fibrous material.

Harvester termites group together at one of the entrance holes to their nest.

An adult Mayfly. Note the long, thread-like tails. This specimen has only two wings and what appears to be two very stunted hindwings. Some species have four wings and three tails.

Mayflies
Order Ephemeroptera

"Ephemero" means short-lived and "ptera" means wings.

The Ephemeroptera is a small order with only about 100 species found in South Africa. Their nymphs are aquatic. Some known as climbers, bottom sprawlers and burrowers occur in quiet ponds while those called clingers are found in fast-moving streams where they cling to rocks or other submerged objects. Mayfly nymphs can be recognised by having usually three but in some species two long tails called cerci at the end of the abdomen.

Adult mayflies are small and dainty insects with a body length of about 10 mm. They have transparent membranous wings which are usually held upright when at rest. Some species have only one pair of wings while others have two. All mayflies have either two or three long threadlike tails. Adults do not have functional mouthparts and do not feed. They usually only live for a few hours during which time they mate. The female lays her eggs in nearby water where they sink to the bottom.

Mayflies are quite unique in that they moult a second time after achieving winged adulthood, despite their short lifetime. They thus have two distinct flying stages, the first known as the subimago and the second as the imago. They are the only insects known to have two flying stages.

A Crab Spider (*Thomisidae* sp.) sits motionless on a flower. They are ambush predators and will wait for a victim to approach before capturing it with their long crab-like forelegs.

Insect spotting

Together with game watching and bird watching, insect spotting is rapidly finding its rightful place as a fascinating and absorbing pastime among an ever-growing number of enthusiasts. While it is an activity that can add a stimulating dimension to a trip to the bush or game reserve, it really requires little in terms of travelling or expenses and can be practised in your own garden, a local park or nearby grassland. It is also a great way to introduce children to the environment. All children are invariably fascinated by insects and it is a pursuit in which children can actively and safely participate.

Recently, in part due to the global warming phenomenon, the scientific community has been placing growing emphasis on the importance of protecting our environmental heritage, some of which is in great danger of being annihilated in the future if counteractive steps are not taken in time. In many instances, this call has been taken up by the media and various interest groups. The public at large has grown significantly more ecology conscious and as a consequence more aware of the natural world about them.

That awareness of environmental matters has truly penetrated the South African scene with its unique and wide-ranging biodiversity can be attested to by the number of wildlife, bird, game, plant, tree and nature books dealing specifically with indigenous fauna and flora that can be seen on the shelves of bookshops of late. In this trend the miniature world of the insect has by no means been overlooked and a number of first-rate field guides dealing with insects and other invertebrates have been published.

But how do you start insect spotting? What special knowledge and what equipment is needed, and just what exactly does insect spotting entail?

Before trying to answer these questions, allow me to point out that at risk of upsetting the entomological establishment, I use the word "insects" with a degree of poetic license throughout this chapter to include any insect-like creatures such as spiders, ticks, centipedes and so on which are not correctly speaking Insecta but members of other groups.

What does insect spotting entail?

Insect spotting, I would say, implies training your eye to see the many tiny entities that have hitherto gone unnoticed. It involves recognising their importance in the food chain and the overall ecology and finally it invariably leads to learning to identify them. What it certainly does not entail is keeping the musty remains of creatures in glass-topped cases or preserved in bottles of alcohol. This is the field of the collector and in my mind should only be practised by institutions such as museums

The head of a small Jumping Spider (*Salticidae* sp.) showing its well-developed eyes. Jumping Spiders are able to "zoom in" on their prey and pounce upon it with great accuracy and speed.

and for scientific or educational purposes. Insects belong in nature where they are able to do the things they were meant to do and not in glass boxes.

Insects form such an integral part of our lives that in fact, with the possible exception of domestic pets, humans live closer to insects than any other living animals. We have become so accustomed to sharing our world with insects that we hardly even notice them, except when they enter our homes or eat our flowers. Yet they are all around us, our gardens and parks are filled with an intriguing abundance of colourful and unusual miniature wildlife ready to be discovered, studied, admired and appreciated.

The tools of the insect spotter

The primary tools of the well-equipped insect spotter include a good field guide for identifying, if only at first to order or family level, the various insects you may see and possibly a note book to jot down your sightings. A magnifying glass or hand lens is valuable for picking up finer detail or observing the smaller species while you can use a small artist's brush to move insects such as bugs or beetles around on foliage without hurting them. Having a digital camera with macro focusing capability is an advantage as you can make permanent records of your sightings.

One or two wide-mouthed transparent plastic bottles are useful for trapping specimens. Use these only for observing the insects which should afterwards be released unharmed. If you are going to keep an insect in a bottle for any length of time, make air holes in the lids. Many insects will also require moisture. You can provide moisture by placing some green grass or damp cotton-wool in the container. However, too much water could cause the insect to drown.

Do keep in mind that some insects such as the Roodepoort Copper Butterfly (*Aloeides dentatis*) are protected while others including certain dung beetles are considered vulnerable and should not be harmed or captured. The various provinces have laws regarding the capture and transportation of insects and in some places a permit is required. These laws and the issuing of permits are, however, so confusing and seem to vary so greatly from province to province and from reserve to reserve that I am unable to give you any valid guidelines.

Binoculars can prove to be useful in insect spotting providing they can focus at a distance of 2 m or closer – not all models can do this. From this distance you can

The beautiful and dainty March Bluetail Damselfly will often be found near garden pools.

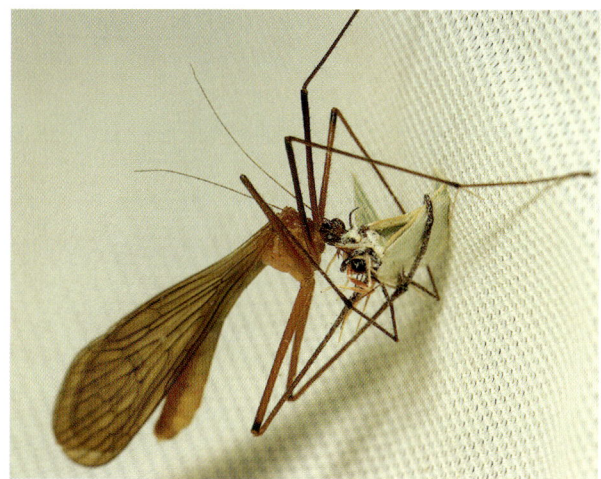

Hangingfly (*Bittacus* sp.) with prey. The Hangingfly belongs to a minor order known as Mecoptera of which there is only one family found in South Africa. They are predacious and feed on small insects and flies which they capture with their long hind legs.

A Grass Stick Insect from the order Phasmatodea.

A Crab Spider (*Thomisidae* sp.) with a captured Honey Bee. The Crab Spider sucks the juices from its prey leaving no more than a husk behind. Its powerful toxin allows it to subdue insects much larger than itself.

watch small insects close-up through the binoculars. If you reverse the binoculars, they act as a low-powered microscope. When using binoculars in this way look through only one barrel.

Where to look for insects

Although there may be thousands of insects in a typical garden, you do need to know where to look to find them. Insects are masters at hiding and camouflage – after all, their very lives often depend on their remaining unseen. Obvious places to start looking are in flower beds or around flowering shrubs or trees. Here you will undoubtedly find honey bees and possibly some wasps foraging for nectar and pollen. The carpenter bee is also a regular visitor to flower beds as are small flower chafer beetles. Tiny crab spiders may also be present. They are fond of sitting on flowers waiting in ambush for other insects to approach. They are rather small, about 4 mm to 5 mm in length and usually a cryptically coloured yellow, pink or green so they need a good eye to spot them. You can easily recognise them by the long crab-like forelegs which they use for capturing their prey.

You may find some of the delicate little leafhoppers on the underside of leaves while the tender young stems of plants are favourite places for sucking bugs such as aphids to gather. These are invariably accompanied by ants.

Several beetles live underground. You can usually detect their presence by observing the leaves of the plant where they would, if present, have left evidence of feeding. Many beetles are nocturnal and feed by night only. They usually climb or fly onto a leaf and start feeding from wherever they land which is often somewhere in the middle of the leaf. Marginal feeding or feeding around the edges of a leaf, on the other hand, usually indicates that larvae or caterpillars have been on the plant. If there is evidence of beetles having fed on plants, you will often find them hiding under the ground near the plant where you may also find beetle larvae and pupae.

Other places where interesting insects may be located are in the forks of trees as well as in any holes or fractures in the bark. Insects often use these natural cavities in which to start a nest or as a safe place to spin a cocoon. You may also find beetles just under the ground at the bases of trees, especially if there is leaf litter lying about. There may also be different types of cockroaches among the leaf litter and if it is moist, woodlouse will invariably be present.

Inspect spider webs carefully as interesting and sometimes out of the ordinary insects often get caught in them. If they have not been there too long they can usually be identified, even if only from their sucked out remains. With a little practice you will be surprised at how quickly you become proficient at spotting insects and other life forms that you have never noticed before.

A garden pool or fish pond is always a popular visiting spot for an assortment of insect life. Many come to drink

A small moth infested with mites. Although mites will often be found on a variety of insects this case is unusual in that the mouthparts of all the mites were imbedded in the proboscis of the moth. No other parts of the moth were affected.

The undersides of leaves will frequently reveal various little creatures, such as these Red Spider Mites (*Tetranychus urticae*).

King Monkey Moth rests on the bark of a tree.

or draw water to build their nests while several lay their eggs either directly in the water or on stones or plants in or surrounding the pond. You may find insect eggs, larvae as well as naiads in the water or living in debris at the bottom of the pond.

Many insects are attracted to light and at night an assortment of insects will always be found sitting close to outdoor lamps. Better yet, you can hang a piece of white linen or an old sheet from a tree branch and place a light at its base. This will attract a variety of insects which will settle on the sheet behind the light. These could include various flies, moths, beetles, mantids, stick insects and antlions as well as some of the tiny and beautiful lacewings that abound in most gardens.

Although a fluorescent light works best as it emits ultraviolet light, any light will do. Energy-saving lights also seem to work well and do not get as hot as conventional globes. A simple light trap can provide a good night's entertainment for the whole family and the children even more than the adults will become highly excited at every new catch that pays a visit.

SEASONALITY AND REGIONAL LOCALITY OF INSECTS

The type and number of insects that can be seen at any particular locality varies from season to season. In early spring or just after the first rains a spate of young larvae and nymphs can be expected as the millions of eggs that have over-wintered under bark, in various crevices or in the ground begin to hatch. They will all be hunting for food so you will seldom have to look further than the nearest clump of foliage to find something of interest.

This is a good time to start keeping a careful watch on one or two nymphs or larvae by checking on them on a regular basis to see how they develop. A piece of fine netting tied around the stem of a plant or a bunch of leaves on which the insects are feeding, will serve to keep your subjects happily confined and enable you to observe their progress as they go through the various stages to reach adulthood.

Insects in general are sensitive to climatic conditions such as humidity and temperature as well as differences between day and night temperatures. These factors influence their life cycles. A butterfly chrysalis which may, for example, take 10 days to develop fully under ideal conditions, could take two or three times as long under different conditions so do not be fooled into thinking that an insect is dead when in fact its development has only been delayed.

Some insects such as certain butterflies, damselflies and dragonflies, are extremely reliant on specific food plants and are consequently only found in certain parts of the country where their host plants are available. The greater majority of insects, however, are not exclusively region bound and can be found throughout the country, although there may be a greater profusion of some species in certain areas where conditions are particularly suited to them. Do not therefore be surprised at finding an insect far from its generally accepted distribution area – this is not unusual.

A final piece of advice in the words of Dr Rob Toms, an eminent entomologist and avid proponent of insect spotting, "Even on a cold winter's morning when there is not a sign of an insect in sight, *remember they are always there.*"

How true this is, for despite the fact that they cannot be seen, they are there, often just in another form. While some insects over-winter and can be found hiding in protected parts of bushes or shrubbery, most will be present in the form of eggs, larvae, pupae or chrysalises. Some may be underground, others attached to twigs by silken threads or tightly rolled up in leaves – but they are there.

SOUTH AFRICA'S BIG 12

Unlike the status given to mammals, fish and birds, South Africa does not as yet have a national insect although entomologists do appear to be thinking along these lines. Hopefully at some stage in the future, with the cooperation of the relevant political authorities, they will come to a decision to honour one of the country's insect species with this status. The idea of adopting a national insect has already been implemented by some countries. Latvia, for example, has as its national insect the beautiful Two-spot Ladybird (*Adalia bipunctata*), in the USA many states have named state insects while discussion is taking place with regard to an American national insect.

At this stage South Africa has taken the lead in another direction and has gone one better. The idea originated from a proposal put forward by Dr Rob Toms, the curator of General Entomology at the Transvaal Museum. A number of eminent entomologists and organisations such as the Entomological Society of South Africa and the Biosystematics Interest Group have collaborated to name and honour a selection of 12 insects with the status of South Africa's Big 12 Insects. The aim is not only to elevate the status of insects to that comparable with the Big 5 mammals, but is also a step towards making entomology and especially insect spotting more user-friendly and acceptable to the public.

Due to the great diversity of the insects, five would have been far too few a number to even begin covering the most important species. Eventually twelve was decided upon as being a representative selection. As individual species are often difficult to identify, this selection has been broadened and generalised to cover similar closely-related species and to facilitate identification by the layperson.

These then are the insects to look out for in the bush, to jot down sightings of, to film and to photograph. Some

A large and ominously coloured centipede. Centipedes are not insects but together with millipedes belong to the superclass Myriapoda.

of them are rarely seen and a good eye is needed to spot others as they are masters at camouflage. To be able to say that all of the Big 12 have been spotted in the wild is an achievement worth noting.

ODONATA

The dragonfly species scientifically known as *Anax tristis* was originally identified as the Giant Dragonfly. However, as this species only occurs in the far northern parts of South Africa and in parts of Zimbabwe, it was decided to include the Blue Emperor Dragonfly (*Anax imperator*) which has a wide distribution in South Africa and is far more readily seen. Blue Emperors are one of our largest dragonflies and can easily reach a length of close to 80 mm with wingspans of 90 mm or more. They are usually found near streams, water pools or slow-flowing rivers, swooping and darting this way and that with great agility as they hunt prey or defend their territory. The male, especially, is an impressive insect with a blue abdomen and a black stripe along its length, apple green thorax and large eyes which almost meet on the top of the head.

BLATTODEA

The Giant Table Mountain Cockroach (*Aptera fusca*) is the second of the Big 12. These interesting insects are limited in distribution to certain areas of the Western Cape where they can be found among fynbos or under rocks on Table Mountain. The fact that they give birth to live young make them especially worthy of note.

Although I have never handled one personally, it is said that they emit a loud squeaking sound when threatened. They are not pests and should not in anyway be compared with the infamous household cockroaches such as the German Cockroach or American Cockroach. Although they belong to the same order they are of a different family. It would indeed be unusual if you ever found *Aptera fusca* in your house.

ISOPTERA

Termites are represented by the large edible Fungus-growing Termite (*Macrotermes* sp.) which also builds some of the largest termitaria in South Africa. Their towering mounds which can exceed 4 m in height are a common feature of the bushveld in the northern areas of the country. They generally feed on dead vegetation which they cover with a plastering of clay. Scratching open a plaster-encrusted dead twig or branch lying in the veld will reveal their presence although they often also forage in the open.

ORTHOPTERA

The large Bladder Grasshoppers, some of which can reach a length of over 100 mm, belong to the family Pneumoridae and are only found in sub-Saharan Africa. Although 17 species have been described in South Africa they are limited in their distribution and can be seen in only a few parts of the country. For this reason any medium to large Bladder Grasshopper is considered representative of one of the Big 12 and can be considered a sighting.

The male Bladder Grasshopper uses his enormous balloon-like body as a natural resonator to amplify the sounds of his shrill stridulations which he produces by rubbing a leg against his abdomen. Bladder Grasshoppers have been said to be among the most spectacular sound-producing insects in the world. Although the male can fly, the female is flightless and needs to make her way along the ground to the loudly serenading male. The hind legs of Bladder Grasshoppers are not enlarged as those of other grasshoppers are, which also renders them incapable of using any meaningful jumping ability.

Bladder Grasshoppers are strongly attracted to light and in the areas in which they are found, may often enter homes. This can attract the males away from a favourable habitat, prevent their mating and result in a depletion of the population. Bladder Grasshoppers are generally green in colour but some species have white or silver dots and markings while others may have red markings.

DIPTERA

Although the Tachinid Fly (*Dejeania bombylans*), also sometimes called a Hedgehog Fly, was originally selected to represent the Diptera order, this has now been replaced by the Spider-wasp Robber Fly (*Proagonistes praeceps*). The decision to do this was based on the fact that *Dejeania* was a seldom seen species and was thus not strongly supported as a member of the Big 12.

The wasp-mimicking Robber Fly is a large insect, mainly black but with an orange head and legs. It is principally found along the coastal areas. Any other large Robber Flies, however, are also acceptable substitutes for sightings. I have discussed Robber Flies in the main section on Diptera and suggest that you refer to this.

I have been unable to further identify this colourful little Tachinid Fly which was found resting on a plant in the late afternoon. But even without a name it remains striking.

Hidden under a strip of bark lay the eggs of an unknown insect.

The dried-out nymphal skin of a cicada remains attached to the bark of a tree after the adult insect has emerged. Although cicada nymphs live underground they surface and climb onto trees for their final moult.

As to the Tachinid Fly it is well worth looking out for in spite of its reduced status. It is a largish yellow fly with black dots down the middle of the upper part of the abdomen and orange splotches on the rear. The body is covered with heavy bristles, hence its common name as a Hedgehog Fly. It also has a pair of fleshy antennae with one prominent bristle and a few smaller ones on each antenna.

Lepidoptera

The Mopane Worm (*Imbrasia belina*) is the undisputed contender for this order. The dried caterpillar of this insect is an important source of protein and a favourite delicacy among many people. I have tried the dried worm on a number of occasions. It is eaten biltong-like and although I found it to be rather dry and bland, I believe it is tasty when fried in oil or made into a stew.

Mopane Worms are widespread in the bushveld areas. The caterpillar is black and covered with little scales of yellow and white which together form bands over the body. It has reddish spines with spiky white hairs.

The large moth, one of the Emperor Moths, is light brown with a large orange eyespot above a broad black and white stripe on each of its hindwings. Like most Emperor Moths it is attracted to light.

Hymenoptera

The Carpenter Bee (*Xylocopa* sp.) from the family Anthophoridae represents this order and has been discussed in the section on Hymenoptera. They are to be found throughout the country and will possibly be one of the first species of the Big 12 to be sighted as they regularly visit gardens.

Mantodea

The Giant Preying Mantis (*Ischnomantis fatilogua*) is the one to look out for among the mantids. It is the longest of the South African mantids and can reach a length of more than 130 mm. Although it can be found over a fairly wide range throughout the country, any large mantid such as the Green Mantid (*Sphodromantis gastrica*) which is more common, can also be accepted as a sighting.

Hemiptera

The Giant Water Bugs (*Lethocerus* sp.) from the family Belostomatidae are one of the largest bugs and also the largest aquatic insects, some reaching close to 80 mm in length. Apart from their conspicuously large size, they can also be recognised by their protruding eyes, snorkel-like breathing tubes at the end of their abdomen and strong forelegs which are adapted to seize and hold prey. They swim with the forelegs stretched forward in readiness to grasp at any approaching victim which include other aquatic insects, tadpoles and even small fish. They can inflict a painful bite with their sharp front beak.

Water bugs can usually be located in shallow pools or quiet areas of streams. Males can sometimes be seen with eggs attached to their backs, placed there by the females. They are also attracted to lamps in the rainy season.

NEUROPTERA

Although the Giant Antlion (*Palpares immensus*) is confirmed as the representative of Neuroptera, any other large species of antlion may be regarded as a sighting. As antlions are discussed in detail in the chapter on Neuroptera no more will be said here.

COLEOPTERA

Coleoptera has two representatives of the order. The Giant Dung Beetle (*Heleocopris andersoni*) was the original choice but the rather unique Addo Flightless Dung Beetle (*Circellium baccus*) which is restricted to the Fish River area in the Eastern Cape and is further listed as a vulnerable species was later added.

PHASMATODEA

Any of the large Stick Insects qualify as one of the Big 12. Stick Insects, some which are up to 300 mm in length, are nocturnal and despite their impressive length are difficult to find during daylight hours. The best way of spotting a Stick Insect is by night when they are active and feeding. They are found in large parts of the country and if you go out during the evening and shine a torch onto trees and shrubs, you may locate one.

In conclusion, a great place to go insect spotting is in any of the many National Botanical Gardens throughout the country. Several botanical gardens have developed a range of different biomes in the gardens, such as wetlands, grasslands and bushveld. These serve to attract a wide spectrum of insect life, each drawn to its preferred habitat.

Early morning or late afternoon is always a good time to observe butterflies, as they are less active than in the heat of the day.

Jumping Spider (*Salticidae* sp.). Size 7 mm.

Digital insect photography

Photographing insects is a highly rewarding pursuit that promises exciting photo prospects for the amateur photographer and also offers many technical and artistic opportunities for the serious nature photographer and environmentalist.

Insects by their very nature and sometimes bizarre appearance, present fascinating and dramatic subject matter for the camera. Adorned with some of nature's most vibrant colours, they are masters of deception, trickery and camouflage. Some boldly flaunt their bright colours, a warning to predators of danger, while others closely resemble dead leaves or multicoloured flowers in their effort to blend in with their natural surroundings. In nature's strange way, some insects are designed to mimic other insects, so we find flies that look like bees, bees that look like wasps and even larvae that look like bird droppings.

This kaleidoscope of nature's incredible diversity is out there just waiting for the photographer's lens to present it to all who would like to experience it. The simple gratification of being able to discover and portray the marvels found in the miniature wonder world of insects is immeasurable. What is more, as the camera often reveals details that normally go unseen by the casual observer, you can always be assured of great interest in your images.

Insect photography embraces a diverse range of subject matter that can include having to photograph anything from stick insects almost 30 cm long to minute springtails only 1 mm in length. Your quest for photographs may at times involve actively stalking your prey through the bush or taking photographs at impossible angles from tree top height to ground level. Sometimes a subject could call for meticulous work in the studio with an elaborate indoor set-up designed to resemble the subject's natural surroundings.

Entomological photography serves not only to provide an endless source of pleasure and pride to the photographer, but can also accomplish an indispensable function in recording and depicting diverse facets of insect life, much of which the average person is not even aware of. The photographer can play an important role in recording new species or species that have migrated from their natural distribution range. Entomologists responsible for documenting insect life often rely on feedback of this nature to supplement their data on certain species.

INSECTS AS SUBJECTS

As any wildlife photographer will confirm, a fundamental prerequisite to taking good wildlife photographs is a first-hand knowledge of the nature of the animals being photographed, such as where they are likely to be found, as well as their habits and behavioural patterns. This concept applies equally to insect photography, which in many respects differs from wildlife photography only in the size of the subject.

Carpenter Bee Robber Fly (*Hyperechia marshalli*) with captured paper wasp (*Polistes fastidiotus*).

Insects have acute hearing, they can sense minute vibrations and have excellent eyesight. Their multifaceted eyes can pick up the slightest movement or change in light. Many are as vigilant as the most nervous buck and most possess the ability to fly. The photographer stalking a skittish butterfly with a camera and long lens capable of only a few centimetres of field depth needs every bit of the skill and dedication of the big game hunter.

Anyone wishing to pursue insect photography must thus of necessity also become involved in the basics of entomology. The insect photographer should at the very least avail him or herself of a good field guide for identifying insects. An understanding of the subject and its characteristics such as behaviour, life cycle and food source, can only lead to better and more meaningful photographs. A number of excellent publications dealing with various facets of insect life as well as identification and classification are available and well worth looking at.

Using digital cameras

In the past close-range work such as insect photography was a relatively restricted field accessible only to the photographer with access to specialised and expensive equipment. The advent of the digital camera has, however, put close-range techniques within the capabilities of most photographers.

Digital cameras using short focal length lenses allow relatively nearby focusing, while most also have a dedicated macro mode, permitting close-up photographs to be taken with ease. Although few of the popular cameras really allow photography in the true macro range, many are quite suitable for photographing most of the larger to medium sized insects.

Insects are remarkably detailed in colour, form and texture and a camera capable of recording at least 4 megapixels or more is necessary to depict this fine detail. Many cameras are also easily and inexpensively adaptable with the addition of a few accessories, to allow much closer or even life-size photos to be taken.

Current technology has served to greatly enhance the scope of the insect photographer and has opened many new innovative opportunities for unusual photographs. The modern digital camera is a marvel of electronic and optical ingenuity. Most models available today can focus and expose automatically, are capable of through-the-lens flash metering and have built-in zoom lenses. Some cameras can take a number of photographs in rapid succession while others come with automatic timing systems, known as intervalometers, which allow time-lapse photographs to be taken over a period of minutes, hours or even days.

The cost of film is also no longer a limiting factor in the number of shots and positions that can be taken of a subject. The instant preview capabilities of both the image and a histogram detailing exposure and tonal range allow the photographer to make an immediate assessment of his or her photographs. This is a great advantage where live, sometimes rapidly-moving insects such as dragonflies or butterflies are being photographed in the field. This type of photography leaves little time for the niceties of precise focusing and often requires that the photograph be taken the instant the image appears sharp in the viewfinder. This can often be a hit and miss affair with possibly more failures than successes, a situation where the capability of on the spot appraisal of the images is an invaluable tool.

To the professional entomologist or serious layperson, digital imaging presents the means of recording, cataloguing and depicting many aspects of their work in a permanent, inexpensive and easily storable form that is immediately compatible with most modern database storage and retrieval systems. Digital photography also allows the interchange of high-quality images for purposes such as classification or confirmation of species to be exchanged worldwide by e-mail, instantly and without the necessity of first having to develop and then scan pictures.

There are several databases and websites currently on the Internet whereby insects can be identified and categorised. These are especially valuable to the photographer, as examples of the work of other nature photographers can be seen and compared. A simple search with the words "insect photography" as keywords reveals an assortment of these sites, many containing valuable information from prominent universities and museums throughout the world.

Although conventional film photography and digital photography both capture images projected through a lens on to a light-sensitive surface with the purpose of producing a final image, usually in the form of a print, this is where the similarity ends. The intermediate steps required to produce the final product differ entirely. Failure to appreciate the intrinsic differences between the two mediums and to adapt working techniques has led to disappointment for many who have made the change to digital imaging.

This state of affairs has been exacerbated by equipment manufacturers and suppliers who like to create the idea that simply by pushing the button you will produce a good photograph. Although this may yield acceptable results to those satisfied with mediocre photos, the discerning photographer who is accustomed to getting the most from the medium will know that this is seldom the case. Those who have been involved with conventional photography will know how important correct darkroom and printing practice is to the final print. The same can be said of digital photography. While the computer has now replaced the darkroom, the basic functions of controlling brightness, contrast, colour balance and tonal quality of the final image are equally important.

This may be a good point at which to discuss the merits, demerits and ethics of digital enhancement and digital manipulation. The sophistication of modern computer graphics software and the ease with which digital images can be manipulated to mislead the viewer has led to a distrust of anything digital as being computer generated. For this reason many photographic competition organisers, for example, hesitate or in some cases even flatly refuse to accept entries of digital photographs, while others require written confirmation that the image has in no way been digitally manipulated. In many cases digital photographs are placed in a category separate from that of conventional photography.

This has led to a school of thought among certain groups of purist photographers that a digital image has no validity unless produced direct from the camera and that any enhancement of the image is unethical. Blatant image manipulation, such as the distortion of the subject or removal or addition of elements within the photograph do have their place in creative photography and in the name of art are quite allowable as such. Where accurate portrayal of the subject matter is considered to be an important element of the photograph such as in insect or other fields of scientific photography, manipulation of the image in any way is naturally unacceptable.

I think we should thus clearly differentiate between manipulation, which suggests engineering of the image in some way, and enhancement which can be considered as presenting the subject matter in the best possible way as regards colour, sharpness, brightness, contrast and tonal qualities of the photograph. The latter, to my way of thinking, is entirely acceptable and even desirable as it follows a process similar to that which would normally be followed during the darkroom processing stages of a conventional photograph.

A QUESTION OF MINDSET

The basic problems faced when venturing into the field of close-range photography are mainly that of having suitable equipment. The camera's optical system must have the ability to function at very close range to record a suitably detailed image of the subject.

Subjects for close-range work can vary in size from small to minute, they can be moving or static, dead or alive, indoors or outdoors. All these factors present the photographer with new problems not normally encountered in everyday photography. Focusing on a 4 mm long, rapidly-moving hover fly, for example, is beyond the bounds of even the best auto-focus lens. It is here where the skill, experience and patience of the photographer come to the fore.

One of the first lessons the aspiring close-range photographer needs to learn involves a total change of mindset, a different way of seeing and experiencing things. We are all used to perceiving the world about us from normal eye level and we see everything in relation to our own size and in terms of our own sense of perspective.

When we start taking photographs at close range, however, subjects inevitably appear different and what was previously no more that an insect sitting on a plant now becomes our prime point of focus. Suddenly we have entered a miniature world where what was previously an insignificant bug now becomes a living creature with large menacing mandibles. In this sense it is not only the relative size of the subject that has changed but also the conditions surrounding it.

It is affected differently by the prevailing light – shadows which may have appeared insignificant or even non-existent from a normal viewing distance now gain importance. A shadow only a few millimetres in size could be sufficient to cover the entire head of our subject and render it too dark. In the same way, highlights take on a new meaning as do other factors such as perspective and composition.

The mindset change involves learning to see in miniature, to think in miniature, to be able to adapt your photographic knowledge and techniques to a miniature world with miniature inhabitants.

TRAIN YOUR BRAIN

Practice serves to train your eye and your brain. Regularly practise studying things close up and from different angles of view. Even when you do not have your camera with you, get down and look closely at leaves, flowers, under leaves and at anything that may lurk there. It will not be long before you find that you are beginning to do

Soldier fly (*Ptecticus elongatus*). Body length ± 6 mm.

this without any conscious effort. You will also soon find that you are beginning to see details that you have never noticed before as well as photo opportunities that you never imagined existed.

Taking mediocre photographs is easy, especially with today's cameras – getting something unique calls for effort and dedication.

Getting to grips with technique

Photographing insects, especially live ones, is never easy but going about it the right way can do much to ensure success. Before embarking on this subject I must point out that I am assuming that you are familiar with the fundamental principles of photography and that you know how to operate your camera, expose, focus, adjust aperture and shutter speed and so on. If not, I strongly suggest you thoroughly study your camera manual or find someone who can help you to the understand the basics.

Macro mode

Digital macro modes, which are often designated by an icon of a tulip on the camera's mode setting dial or button, allow much closer focusing than would normally be the case. However, it must be appreciated that digital macro modes never really approach true macrophotography which refers to taking photographs at life size or what is known as a 1:1 magnification ratio or greater. Although macro modes may allow quite sufficient magnification for many subjects, it can be limiting when you wish to photograph smaller subjects such as some insects. Most digital macro modes restrict the photographer to photographing the larger insects such as grasshoppers, butterflies or beetles.

More advanced single lens reflex (SLR) cameras have many ways of getting around this limitation as extension tubes, bellows or tele-extenders can easily be added between the camera and lens allowing for extreme close-ups, while dedicated macro lenses can also be fitted.

Fixed-lens cameras, on the other hand, limit you to adding optics to the front of the lens only. However, as digital cameras allow unlimited experimentation without having to waste expensive film, various optical combinations to decrease camera-to-subject distance can easily be tested.

Things you can try are magnifying glasses, loupes, binocular or telescope front lenses and even spectacle lenses. These can be taped to the front of the camera lens and should all serve to facilitate closer focusing and greater subject/image magnification. In fact, I often use the front end of a pair of binoculars as a supplementary lens and get excellent results.

Commercially available supplementary lenses as described below can also be fitted. Any camera that has threads on the front of the lens barrel to accept filters will also accept supplementary lenses of the appropriate size.

Supplementary lenses

Supplementary or close-up lenses as they are sometimes called, are by far the cheapest and simplest way of decreasing your camera-to-subject distance. Similar in many ways to the optics used in spectacles to counteract far-sightedness, supplementary lenses allow the camera to focus on close objects. Like filters they screw into the front of the camera lens and do not require the lens to be removed from the camera. They are thus suitable for use on prosumer and other fixed-lens digital cameras providing the camera has filter threads on the front of the lens. If your camera has a macro mode setting the use of supplementary lenses combined with the camera's macro setting will permit focusing of close to 1:1.

Supplementary lenses are fitted to the front of the camera lens and offer an inexpensive way of equipping a camera for close-up photography.

Supplementary lenses are measured in diopters. The higher the diopter number is, the stronger the lens is and consequently the closer it will allow the camera to focus. Normally sold in sets of three lenses of +1, +2 and +4 diopters, they can be used individually or stacked to decrease the focus distance still further. A +1 and a +4 diopter lens together will give +5 diopters and so on. When stacking, it is important to always place the highest diopter number lens on the camera lens and then follow up with the next highest number, with the weakest being placed last. They do not affect exposure so no light is lost through their use, while all the camera's normal functions such as TTL light metering, auto flash and auto focus will also remain functional.

Although supplementary lenses offer many advantages as regards cost and simplicity of use and would appear to be the

The top photograph was taken at 150 mm from the subject, using the closest focusing distance allowed by the camera's macro mode. For the photo above a combination of +1, +2 and +4 supplementary lenses were added, giving a total of +7 diopters. This reduced the focusing distance to 70 mm allowing for increased magnification of the subject.

perfect answer to getting closer, they also have their downside. Most simple single-element supplementary lenses display colour fringing. This is caused by their inability to focus light waves of different lengths at the same point and results in the image showing a number of spectrum-like colours fringing the edges. This can usually be corrected by the use of multiple-element supplementary lenses which are made by some camera manufacturers. These are in a considerably higher price range than single-element supplementary lenses but are well worth the additional expense. The number of glass-to-air surfaces that is caused by stacking supplementary lenses can also have a detrimental effect on the sharpness of the image as light reacts differently in the different mediums. Experimentation is the keyword.

To sum up, supplementary lenses offer an easy and inexpensive way to get closer. Despite what has been said above, the loss of image quality and sharpness is generally minimal and will go unnoticed with most subjects except the most critical. Colour fringing usually only becomes apparent with subjects which have large monochromatic areas or backgrounds, and sharpness can always be slightly enhanced with the use of most image processing software applications.

Extension tubes

If your camera is of the single lens reflex type which allows you to use interchangeable lenses, extension tubes, which are in fact just spacers as they have no glass elements, can be fitted between the camera and lens to allow for close focusing. Extension tubes need to be compatible with your camera to permit the camera's full automatic focusing and exposure control to function. Most major camera manufacturers make extension tubes for their cameras, often obtainable either singly or in a set of three.

Tubes give good results and sharpness and can be stacked allowing very close-range macrophotography. Final quality will always be dependent on the quality of the lens used with the tubes.

Extension tubes do have a few drawbacks. Firstly, as they extend the lens quite considerably if a number of tubes are stacked, they make a camera unwieldy and difficult to hold steady. The use of stacked extension tubes invariably requires the use of a sturdy tripod. Secondly, they cut the light reaching the digital sensor requiring more exposure which needs to be compensated for either by lowering the camera's shutter speed or by using a larger aperture. Both these options have their disadvantages as a slow shutter speed increases the possibility of camera shake while larger apertures decrease depth-of-field.

Everything that I have said above also applies to bellows, which are no more than variable length extension tubes.

Reversed 50 mm

Bona fide macrophotography, often also called photomacrography, refers to photographs taken at life size or greater magnifications. The *Focal Encyclopaedia of Photography* puts it as follows: "Macrophotography is the process of taking larger-than-life photographs with ordinary camera lenses. Macrophotography ends and photomicrography (with microscope lenses) begins, at about 10× diameters."

The difference between the actual size of the subject and the image size is designated by their relation to each other. For example, a 1:1 ratio refers to a life-size image, 1:2 is an image half life size and 2:1 is double life size.

To achieve magnifications larger than life size, special macro lenses are available which have been specially designed for this purpose. Due to their optical complexity, true macro lenses are notoriously expensive and will usually only be found in the arsenal of the professional.

Few aspiring macrophotographers, however, realise that they probably have lying about in the back of some cupboard a highly sophisticated, highly corrected macro lens just waiting to be used. What I am talking about is the standard 50 mm lens from a (now obsolete?) 35 mm SLR film camera. These lenses are also readily available from second-hand dealers or swap shops for next to nothing. I recently purchased two at under R50 each. The standard 50 mm lens has been designed for long lens-to-subject distances (infinity) and a short lens to film distance (focal length). In macrophotography, however, these conditions are reversed and the lens-to-subject distance needs to be less than the lens-to-film distance to attain the desired degree of magnification of the subject. It only makes good sense therefore to reverse the lens to achieve this.

The shorter the focal length of the lens is, the greater is the magnification that can be achieved. A 28 mm lens for instance will allow you to get considerably closer than a 50 mm lens. The shorter focal length lenses, however, do present other problems such as vignetting or darkening of the edges of the image so we will stay with the 50 mm lens for the moment.

A reversed lens can be fitted directly onto the front of virtually any fixed or zoom lens. This is known as stacking. When an SLR camera with a removable lens is used, the reversed lens can also be used with a bellows unit or extension tubes only. When lenses are stacked the resulting increase in glass and air surfaces does cause a slight degrading of image quality. Thus if your equipment allows it the latter method will produce better definition. On the other hand, the quality loss through stacking is relatively small and this method offers many other advantages.

When stacking, all the functions of your fixed lens such as exposure control and auto focus can still be fully used. These functions fall away when the lens is used with extension tubes only. Even if you are using dedicated extension tubes they will not be operative on the reversed lens.

Fitting the reversed lens is a simple operation. Although reversal rings are made by some manufacturers they are difficult to obtain and anyway the chances are great that the lens to be reversed will differ from the lens on your camera if you are stacking and you probably will not find a ring that fits both lenses. In fact, it is probably easier making your own from the outset.

You are going to need two filter rings or step-up or step-down rings, one to fit the front of your fixed lens and one to fit the front of the supplementary lens that is to be reversed. These rings now need to be glued together back-to-back. Superglue works fine although I find that two-part resin glue or paste gives a firmer bond. When gluing be sure that the two rings are accurately centred. Now all that is needed is to screw the two lenses together front to front.

Keep in mind that only the optics of the supplementary lens are needed when the lenses are stacked. The aperture of the supplementary lens must thus be fully opened and the lens focused on infinity. Exposure and focus are controlled by the master fixed lens.

When a reversed lens is attached to extension tubes or bellows, the aperture of the reversed lens is used for exposure while movement of the bellows focuses the lens. When using fixed extension tubes, focus is obtained by moving the camera backwards or forwards. The focusing mechanism on the reversed lens itself will have almost no effect and for best results should be left on infinity.

When lenses are stacked, the focal length of the master lens needs to be long enough to accommodate the supplementary lens. Its field of view needs to be narrow enough so as not to record an area larger than the maximum aperture opening of the supplementary lens or vignetting will occur. If the camera's fixed lens has zooming capabilities, zoom in at least to the point where no darkening of the edges can be seen. With a 50

A 50 mm lens fitted to a camera which has a fixed (non-interchangeable) zoom lens.

Two filter rings can be glued together to form a very functional reversal adaptor for a 50 mm lens.

mm reversed supplementary lens a 100 mm lens or a lens zoomed to the equivalent of 100 mm works perfectly. If a lens with a shorter focal length than 50 mm is used as the supplementary, a correspondingly longer master lens is needed. While on the question of lenses it is worth noting that prime lenses (lenses of a fixed focal length) deliver considerably better results when used as master lenses than do zoom lenses.

The possible degree of magnification using stacked lenses is also quite straightforward to determine. In our example above where a 100 mm lens is used in conjunction with a reversed 50 mm lens you will get a magnification of 100 divided by 50, or ×2 or put another way 2:1. In the same way a 200 mm master lens combined with a 28 mm supplementary will give you a 7:1 magnification.

Unless you are using specialist equipment specially designed for macrophotography, be prepared to experiment. Accessories for adapting standard cameras for macro purposes are both scarce and highly priced. However, you will be surprised what can be achieved with various makeshift methods using an assortment of lenses, masking tape, prestick and glue.

Exposure

Broadly speaking, exposure technique in close-range work is no different than that of any other type of photography. To clarify, you need to obtain a balance between the amount of light reflected from the subject, the sensitivity of the digital sensor (ISO/film speed setting), the amount of light allowed to enter the camera (aperture) and the time that the light is allowed to fall on the sensor (shutter speed). Properly controlled, these four factors result in a correctly exposed photograph, one that has sufficient detail in shadows, mid-tones and highlights.

All cameras these days have sophisticated built-in exposure measuring systems and generally take care of all these factors, including the necessary exposure compensation required for extension tubes or sundry filters.

Insect photography, however, does present situations with which the camera's auto exposure system cannot deal. We may, for example, have a dark-coloured insect resting on a light flower or conversely a light-coloured insect on dark foliage or, as very often happens, an insect on a flower or leaf with dark shadowed vegetation in the background. In spite of the fact that many manufacturers have developed methods that try to overcome these kinds of problems, such as centre-weighted exposure measurement, they are often unable to cope with the extreme contrast you may encounter in some situations. It is necessary for the photographer to recognise this and take the necessary steps such as bracketing exposures or taking photos at one F-stop over exposure and one at an F-stop under as well as the normal exposure as given by the camera.

Insects themselves as subjects are problematic. Some dark-coloured insects are so dark that they reflect almost no light and additional exposure, even at the expense of overexposing the background must often be given to obtain any detail at all of the insect's body.

Many insects such as beetles as well as other families have a coating of wax which produces very strong reflections and highlights capable of confusing any camera's exposure system. To give an example, photographing an insect like an Oriental Cockroach which is densely black and very shiny, requires about two F-stops or four times normal exposure to obtain any surface detail. This is normally only the case when photographing certain live insects for after death the wax layer on the insect's body slowly dries and presents less of a problem. People who photograph dead insects regularly for entomological or museum collections, should dip the subject in alcohol or soapy water to remove the waxy coating before photographing it.

Reversed lens stacked on a 100 mm macro lens.

For beginners the best way of getting around most of these problems is to take plenty of photographs, try different exposures and different positions. I strongly advise you to keep notes on what you have done, your different exposures, type of prevalent lighting, for example, shadow, overcast or strong sunlight. This will prove invaluable at a later stage when you study your photographs on a computer screen and can then compare what you have done with the various images.

As you become more experienced you will begin to immediately recognise those subjects that require more exposure and those that require less. Do keep in mind that the digital medium is much like colour slides when it comes to exposure. A degree of underexposure can be tolerated but overexposure causes blooming and burning out of highlights and overexposed shots can rarely be used or corrected.

Depth-of-field

Depth-of-field is such an important factor in close-range and macrophotography that it demands a full discussion. Depth-of-field refers to that area which, from close to the lens to further away, is rendered sharply. You may, for instance, find that the head of an insect on which you have focused is sharp while its rear end is completely out of focus. This range of sharp (or fuzzy) focus can be controlled and is dependent on a number of factors:

- The longer the focal length of the lens or the more you have zoomed it in, the less depth-of-field you will have.
- Closely approaching a subject reduces depth-of-field and it becomes critical in macrophotography where the camera may be only centimetres from the subject. In some cases depth may be limited to only a few millimetres.
- The larger the aperture setting on your camera is, the less the depth-of-field is. The smaller the aperture is, the more the depth-of-field is.
- Depth-of-field is always greater beyond the point of focus than before it.

The first two points are usually predetermined when photographing insects. After all, you will want to use maximum zoom while getting as close as possible to fill the frame with the subject.

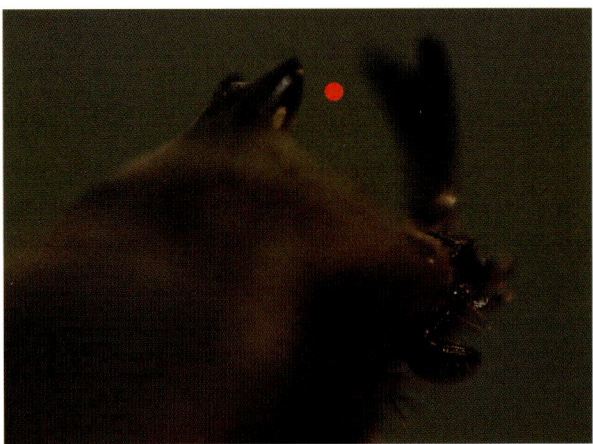

An illustration of depth-of-field. The two horns of this rhino beetle were 5 mm apart; focusing on either would render the other one out of focus. The camera was thus manually focused on an imaginary point between the horns, here illustrated by the red dot. At F2.8 the entire image appears out of focus.

The third, the aperture, offers you a degree of control over the depth-of-field. Ideally, you should use the smallest possible aperture and so obtain the greatest depth-of-field. However, bear in mind that the smaller the aperture is set, the slower the shutter speed needs to be set to compensate for the reduced light now entering the camera. Slow shutter speeds invariably result in camera shake and blurred subjects unless the camera is supported by a sturdy tripod, which is not always practical in the field. You can compensate for this by using a higher ISO/film speed but high ISO speeds also result in degradation of image quality due to noise which is amplified in the digital sensor.

Stopping down to f32 increases the depth-of-field to the extent where both horns are in focus.

The answer then is to try to find a happy medium between these various factors by using the smallest aperture possible while still maintaining a reasonably fast shutter speed and a low to medium ISO/film speed setting. In bright sunlight this may be something like the following:
- Film speed: 200 ISO
- Shutter speed: 1/200 second
- Aperture: F11 or F16.

Using a flash

Low light conditions such as in shadowed areas or at dusk, require the use of a flash to supplement the available lighting. The on-camera flashes fitted to many cameras are of little use in close-range photography as their light will be thrown either over or to the side of the subject, depending on where it is placed on the camera. This varies from camera to camera depending on the angle of illumination of the flash.

It is a good idea to carry out a few tests to determine the minimum distance that your flash will evenly illuminate a subject before you try any serious work. To conduct these tests set up a static subject, any small object will do, preferably indoors where it will not receive too much ambient light. Set your flash on and take a series of photographs at decreasing distances from the subject. A study of the results will quickly show the minimum distance at which the flash is no longer able to illuminate the full frame.

For serious close-range work an off-camera flash that can be removed from the camera and aimed directly at the subject is needed. Special ring-light flashes which fit over the camera's lens or miniature twin flashes are specially designed for this purpose. They are specialised items of equipment and are generally costly. An ordinary off-camera flash can be quite successfully employed providing some sort of bracket is used to hold the flash so that its light is directed downwards to fall just in front of the lens. If a dedicated flash designed for use on your particular camera is used the camera's auto exposure system should take care of the flash exposure.

Colour balance

Modern digital cameras are all fitted with an automatic colour balance mode which measures the colour of the light entering the camera and then makes the necessary adjustments to neutralise any colour casts. Daylight, for example, is close to white but the exact colour varies according to the time of day. Tungsten light, on the other hand is red, while fluorescent light is bluish greenish.

Like automatic exposure meters, auto colour balance can easily be fooled into filtering out the wrong colours. Take, for instance, a full frame shot of a bug sitting on a yellow daisy. The camera's auto colour balance will sense this as having a predominance of yellow as reflected off the daisy which will take up most of the background, and will attempt to compensate by removing yellow and adding the opposite colour which is blue. The result is that the colour of both the insect and the daisy will be rendered incorrectly as yellow has now been removed.

To render the insect as accurately as possible it is advisable to switch off the automatic colour balance function. To do this set the camera's colour balance on Daylight, usually indicated by an icon of the sun. In my opinion this by far gives the most consistent and accurate colour rendition of subjects under any daylight conditions. Obviously if photographs are being taken indoors with the use of tungsten light the camera needs to be set on Tungsten, usually indicated by an icon of an electric light globe.

Scanning insects

Both these images have been made using a standard flatbed scanner. Hindwing of Veld Antlion (*Palpares* sp.); Forewing of Veld Antlion (*Palpares* sp.)

Using a flatbed scanner to record images of various small dead insects or insect parts such as wings is a technique that is often used and that can deliver surprisingly good results. The procedure is simple and quick. The insect is simply placed on the scanner platen as you would a document, cropped to include only the required area and the scanner activated. Scans should be made in full colour or greyscale at a minimum of 300 dpi.

It may well be necessary to make adjustments to the contrast and density settings of the scanner to obtain correct exposures if your scanner software allows for this. A little experimentation with each subject is usually called for to obtain the best results. Colour saturation can also be increased to brighten up the colours. As a scanner lights an image from the bottom from under the glass, the subject should be placed with the surface to be scanned downwards.

Scanners have no depth-of-field and the subject must be held flat against the glass. A little additional pressure can be placed on the scanner cover to ensure good contact with the scanner glass. A book placed on the cover works well, although care should be taken not to squash delicate insects.

Scanners work especially well to record wing patterns and wing venation of various insects. The wings of many insects such as moths and butterflies are made up of numerous small scales while many other

The minuteness of this little Braconid wasp can be measured against the size of the thorns, which gives a sense of scale to the photograph.

insects have microscopic hairs on the wings. These can easily be dislodged during scanning and remain behind on the scanner's glass causing them to show up on the next scan. Thorough cleaning of the glass is thus essential after each scan.

Tripods

A tripod is often the last piece of equipment most aspiring photographers consider investing in. Yet in close-range photography it can prove to be one of the most essential pieces of equipment in your photographic arsenal.

Conditions which clearly demand the use of a tripod are when photographs are taken in low light, such as in shadow or during the early morning or at dusk. Other compelling reasons for using a tripod are when strong telephoto or zoom lenses are used or the camera is set at a very low shutter speed. Photographers often consider these situations as being the only times a tripod is of value. However, it is a fact that the sharpness of most photographs, regardless of the prevailing light or shutter speed, can be improved by the use of a tripod or other means of supporting the camera.

When taking close-range photographs, camera movement is without doubt possibly the single most common reason for disappointing results. Often put down to lack of depth-of-field, bad focus, an inferior lens or a multitude of other reasons, fuzzy photographs are often the result of the camera being moved, however slightly, at the moment of taking the photograph. In cases where extensive camera movement has taken place it is quite obvious and easily recognised by the blurring of all lines in one direction. When only a small degree of camera movement has taken place it can result in no more than a slight softening of the image but enough to render the image fuzzy.

The closer you get to a subject, the more critical camera movement becomes. The close-range photographer should thus consider a tripod as not just a useful but rather an essential piece of equipment to be used whenever circumstances allow.

Although a tripod is the ideal tool for stabilising the camera, it is not always practical to use in the field, especially when photographing live subjects such as insects. Setting up a tripod, adjusting the legs and fitting the camera takes time during which your insect could decide it no longer wants to be photographed and depart to better places. In situations such as these a monopod, which is an apparatus with only one adjustable leg on which the camera is fitted, is often more useful.

Selecting a tripod

A fact of life is that not all tripods are created equal, hence the great difference in price range between various makes and models. Although a bad tripod may arguably be better than no tripod at all, what is ideally needed is a sturdy, rigid piece of equipment that can be rapidly and easily set up and which allows for quick attachment and precise alignment of your camera. Unfortunately, the sturdier the tripod is, the heavier it is and the more it costs. The ideal is to select a tripod that suits your particular needs so that while being sturdy it is also practical to carry around, sometimes for hours at a time in the field. Even the very best tripod will invariably be left behind if it proves to be too heavy or cumbersome.

Before buying a tripod check out the following:
- Twist test. Set the tripod up with its legs fully extended. Without a camera attached, press down on the tripod head and twist to the left and right. If the legs allow the tripod to be twisted, even a little, consider it as being unsuitable. The legs should be strong enough or strengthened by bracing brackets to withstand any twist.
- The telescopic legs must be easily adjustable and should lock firmly. They should be able to withstand a reasonable amount of weight without sliding back in or buckling.
- What type of locks do the legs have? Clip locks work fine and are usually faster to operate than twist locks. Just make sure that they lock and release easily and smoothly. If the legs have twist locks check that these can be released easily. Twist locks are notorious for locking-up, requiring the use of both hands and sometimes herculean strength to release.

- Extend the centre post if the tripod is fitted with one. This should also lock firmly, should not wobble even at full extension and above all should not slide down when weight is placed on it. If the centre post is operated by a crank this should also be smooth operating and be capable of heightening or lowering the post in small increments.
- The head. While some manufacturers incorporate the tripod head as part of the tripod others require that you buy it as a separate accessory. Either way the tripod head is an extremely important component and should be looked at carefully. The head should operate very smoothly and allow small adjustments to tilt and swing without any jerkiness. This is vitally important in close-range photography as any stickiness in the head's tilt adjustment could cause your camera to jump from one position to the next, when what is required is a smooth movement. Heads with so-called fluid movement are the best. Ball heads also work very well providing they meet the requirements of smooth fluid operation as described above.
- Finally you need to look at how the camera is attached to the head. Screw-type heads allow the camera body to be screwed directly onto the tripod via the tripod fitting at the bottom of

The tympanic organs (ears) of a grasshopper are situated on the first segment of the abdomen. Here enough of the insect has been included to allow the viewer to judge the size of the organ against other body parts of the grasshopper.

the camera. Although slower to use than other methods, screw fittings ensure a firm fitting with no play between camera and tripod. Quick-release fittings incorporate a dovetailed shoe or female fitting on the tripod head and a corresponding male fitting on the camera. While some work well, others do not always lock the camera securely into place. I have also found that many of the so called quick-release mechanisms on tripods require such precise alignment of the shoe and release clip before the camera can be fitted or removed that they are more of a hindrance than a help.

Monopods

Monopods are an excellent alternative for use in the field. Obviously, having only one leg, they are not nearly as sturdy as a good tripod but on the other hand they are not as heavy either and are a lot quicker and easier to set up. Everything that I have said above relating to the selection of a tripod applies equally well to a monopod.

Monopods do require some practice in their use as they are supported by only a single leg. The photographer has to learn to place a little downward pressure on the camera to fully stabilise them and above all not to allow the camera to sway to either side or backwards or forwards. A monopod should not be considered a replacement for a tripod but rather as a substitute when the use of a tripod is not practical.

Whatever you decide to use, the important thing is to ensure that whenever possible your camera is stabilised. A tree trunk, a rock, the bumper of your car, virtually anything that you can rest your camera on or hold it against will help.

Some final words of advice

In conclusion allow me to point out that technique is not the be all and end all of good photography. A photograph showing action, such as an insect capturing its prey, moulting, laying eggs or doing any of the many things that insects do can have greater value, even if a little blurred or lacking depth-of-field, than a perfectly sharp static image which conveys nothing of the insect itself.

It is also good practice when photographing an insect close up to always move back a little and, if possible, take a second photograph depicting its surroundings such as the vegetation or host plant on which it may be feeding.

Always record sufficient images when an opportunity presents itself and rather take too many than too few photographs. With digital media the cost of film is no longer a factor so if the subject allows it take shots at different exposure settings, with and without a flash. Try different angles and different distances from the subject. This is especially important if you are a beginner as it is the only way that you will learn. Even if it does mean having to delete 90% of your work, this is fine. As you progress your eye will become more trained and you will become more familiar with your camera. Soon you will find that you need to take fewer and fewer shots to get a good final photograph.

A final word of advice – always have your camera at the ready. You will often find the most interesting subjects in the strangest places and at the most unexpected times.

A young Hairy Field Spider emerging from its silken egg case. Inclusion of the egg case, as well as the dry leaves in which it was encased adds interest and meaning to the photograph.

Insect orders

Certain minor orders have been omitted as they are either of little importance or will not be found in South Africa.

Archeognatha – Bristletails
Blattodea – Cockroaches
Coleoptera – Beetles
Collembola – Springtails
Dermaptera – Earwigs
Diplura – Diplurans
Diptera – Flies
Embioptera – Web spinners
Ephemeroptera – Mayflies
Hemiptera – Bugs
Hymenoptera – Ants, bees, wasps
Isoptera – Termites
Lepidoptera – Butterflies, moths
Mantodea – Mantids
Mantophasmatodea – Heel-walkers
Mecoptera – Hangingflies
Megaloptera – Dobsonflies, alderflies
Neuroptera – Lacewings, antlions
Odonata – Dragonflies, damselflies
Orthoptera – Grasshoppers, crickets, katydids
Phasmatodea – Stick insects
Phthiraptera – Lice
Plecoptera – Stoneflies
Psocoptera – Booklice
Siphonaptera – Fleas
Strepsiptera – Stylops
Thysanoptera – Thrips
Thysanura – Silverfish
Trichoptera – Caddisflies

Insect names English/Afrikaans

Alderflies – Bergstroomjuffers
Antlions – Mierleeus
Ants – Miere
Aphids – Plantluise
Assassin bugs – Roofwantse
Backswimmers – Rugswemmers
Bagworms – Sakwurms
Bark beetles – Baskewers
Bed bugs – Weeluise
Bee flies – Byvlieë
Bees – Bye
Beetles – Kewers
Blowflies – Brommers
Booklice – Boekluise
Brush-footed butterflies – Borselpootskoenlappers
Bugs – Besies
Caddisflies – Kokerjuffers
Carpenter bees – Houtbye
Checkered beetles – Bontroofkewers
Cicadas – Sonbesies
Click beetles – Kniptorre
Clothes moths – Kleremotte
Cockroaches – Kakkerlakke
Cotton stainers – Rooiwantse
Crane flies – Langpote
Crickets – Krieke
Cuckoo wasps – Koekoekwespe
Damselflies – Waterjuffers
Darkling beetles – Skemerkewers
Diving beetles – Waterkewers
Dragonflies – Naaldekokers
Dung beetles – Miskruiers
Earwigs – Oorkruipers
Emperor moths – Pouoë
Fireflies, glow worms – Glimwurms
Fleas – Vlooie
Flesh flies – Vleisvlieë
Flies – Vlieë
Grasshoppers – Sprinkane
Ground beetles – Grondkewers
Hawk moths – Pylsterte
Honey bees – Heuningbye
Horse flies – Blindevlieë
House flies – Huisvlieë

Hover flies – Sweefvlieë
Katydids – Langhoringsprinkane
Lacewings – Netvlerkies
Ladybird beetles – Skilpadjies
Leaf beetles – Blaarvreetkewers
Leafcutter bees – Blaarsnybye
Leafhoppers – Blaarspringers
Lice – Luise
Long-horn beetles – Langhoringkewers
Loopers – Landmeters
Mantids – Hotnotsgotte
Mayflies – Eendagvlieë
Midges – Muggies
Mole crickets – Molkrieke
Mosquitoes – Muskiete
Moth flies – Motvlieë
Net-winged beetles – Platvlerkkewers
Owl moths – Uilmotte
Plant bugs – Plantwantse
Plume moths – Veermotte
Potter wasps – Pleisterperdebye
Redheaded flies – Rooikopvlieë
Rhinoceros beetles – Renosterkewers
Robber flies – Roofvlieë
Rove beetles – Dwaalkewers
Sawflies – Bladwespe
Scale insects – Dopluise
Scorpionflies – Skerpioenvlieë

Seed weevils – Boontjiekewers
Shield bugs – Skildstinkbesies
Silverfish – Vismotte
Skin beetles – Velkewers
Snout bugs – Lanternbesies
Snout weevils – Snuitkewers
Spider-hunting wasps – Spinnekopjagters
Spittle bugs – Skuimbesies
Stalk-eyed flies – Steeloogvlieë
Stick insects – Stokinsekte
Stoneflies – Pêrelvlieë
Swallowtails – Swaelsterte
Termites – Termiete
Thick-headed flies – Dikkopvlieë
Thrips – Blaaspootjies
Tiger beetles – Sandkewers
Tiger moths – Tiermotte
Treehoppers – Boomspringers
Tsetse flies – Tsetsevlieë
Twig wilters – Blaarpootwantse
Velvet ants – Fluweelmiere
Wasps – Perdebye
Water boatmen – Bootmannetjies
Water scorpions – Waterskerpioene
Water striders – Waterlopers
Web-spinners – Tonnelspinners
Whirligig beetles – Waterhondjies

Source: Braack L. *Field Guide to the Insects of the Kruger National Park.* Struik Publishers. Cape Town.

Pronunciation of insect families

Aphididae – ay-**phid**-di-dee
Apidae – **ay**-pi-dee
Asilidae – ah-**sill**-li-dee
Bombyliidae – bomb-bi-**lye**-i-dee
Calliphoridae – cal-li-**phor**-ri-dee
Carabidae – ca-rab-**bi**-dee
Cerambycidae – cer-am-**bis**-si-dee
Cercopidae – ser-**cope**-pi-dee
Cetoniinae – si-**toni**-i-nee
Cicadellidae – sic-cah-**dell**-li-dee
Coccinellidae – cock-si-**nel**-li-dee
Coreidae – co-**ree**-i-dee
Culicidae – coo-**liss**-si-dee
Curculionidae – cur-cool-lee-**on**-nih-dee
Diopsidae – diop-**si**-dee
Dytiscidae – dy-**tis**-ci-dee
Eumenidae – eu-**men**-i-dee
Fulgoridae – full-go-**ree**-dee
Hesperiidae – hess-per-**rye**-i-dee
Lycaenidae – lye-**seen**-ni-dee
Lycidae – ly-**si**-dee
Margodidae – mar-**god**-i-dee
Meloidae – mel-**low**-i-dee
Membracidae – mem-**bra**-ci-dee
Noctuidae – noc-**too**-i-dee
Nymphalidae – nym-**phal**-li-dee
Papilionidae – pah-pill-li-**on**-ni-dee
Pentatomidae – pen-ta-**tom**-mi-dee
Pieridae – pi-**air**-ri-dee
Psychidae – si-**kie**-dee
Psychodidae – **psycho**-di-dee
Reduviidae – reh-deu-**vie**-i-dee
Sarcophagidae – sar-co-**pha**-gi-dee
Scarabaeidae – scare-ah-**bee**-i-dee
Sesiidae – se-**si**-i-dee
Sphingidae – sphin-**gi**-dee
Syrphidae – **sear**-phi-dee
Tachinidae – ta-**kin**-ni-dee
Tenebrionidae – teh-knee-bree-**on**-ni-dee
Tephritidae – tef-**rit**-ti-dee
Vespidae – **vess**-pi-dee
Xylocopinae – zilo-**cop**-pi-nee

REFERENCES

As an amateur entomologist I have had to depend strongly on a number of sources from experts in various fields. Many thanks to the authors and publishers for the following excellent works from which I could source information.

Braack L. *Field Guide to the Insects of the Kruger National Park*. Struik Publishers. Cape Town.
Bullough W.S. *Practical Invertebrate Anatomy*. Macmillan & Co. London.
Filmer M.R. *Southern African Spiders*. Struik Publishers. Cape Town.
Grimaldi D., Engel M.S. *Evolution of the Insects*. Cambridge University Press. New York.
Holm E., Marais E. *Fruit Chafers of Southern Africa*. Ekogilde. Hartbeespoort.
Imes R. *The Practical Entomologist*. Aurum Press. London.
Leroy A. & J. *Spiderwatch in Southern Africa*. Struik Publishers. Cape Town.
Migdoll I. *Veldgids tot die Skoenlappers van Suider-Afrika*. Struik Publishers. Cape Town.
Oldroyd H. *Collecting, Preserving and Studying Insects*. Anchor Press. Essex.
Picker M., Griffiths C., Weaving A. *Field Guide to Insects*. Struik Publishers. Cape Town.
Scholtz C. H., Holm E. *Insects of Southern Africa*. Butterworth Publishers. Durban.
Skaife S.H. *African Insect Life*. Struik Publishers. Cape Town.
Skaife S.H. *The Study of Ants*. Longmans, Green & Co. London.
Tarboton W. & M. *A Field Guide to the Damselflies of South Africa*. Privately published.
Vesey-Fitz Gerald B. *The Worlds of Ants, Bees and Wasps*. Pelham Books. London.
Woodhall S. *Field Guide to the Butterflies of South Africa*. Struik Publishers. Cape Town.

Internet sources

Australian Museum: www.amonline.net.au/insects/
Commonwealth Scientific and Industrial Research Organisation (CSIRO): www.csiro.au/
Ecoport: www.ecoport.org/
Iowa State University of Science and Technology: www.ent.iastate.edu/
Lamberts Smith's Insecta: www.insecta.co.za
Iziko Museums of Cape Town: www.museums.org.za/bio/insects/
North Carolina State University NC State University: www.cals.ncsu.edu
Science in Africa: www.scienceinafrica.co.za/
Transvaal Museum: www.nfi.org.za/tmpage.html
University of Kentucky, College of Agriculture: www.ca.uky.edu/

INDEX

Bold numbers indicate photographs.

A

abdomen 13, 14
Acanthaspis sp. **46**
Acraea sp. **86**
Acrida acuminata **135, 142**
Acrididae 139
Acrotylus sp. **141**
Addo Flightless Dung Beetle 180
African Humming Bird Moth **96, 97**
African Killer Bees 69
African Mole Cricket **147**
African Monarch **91**
African Thief Ant **66**
Agaristidae 95
Agdistis sp. **94**
Agonoscelis versicolor **42**
Allodapula variegata **67**
Allograpta **28**
Allograpta sp. **27**
Aloeides dentatis 81, 173
Ambush Bugs **46**
American Cockroach **161, 163**
Amethyst Fruit Chafer 11, **107, 118**
Ammophila sp. **77**
Anax imperator 177
Anax tristis 177
Anisoptera 153
Anisorrhina flavomaculata **106, 117**
Anisorrhina sp. **117, 118**
Anostostomatidae 145
ant larvae **65**
antennae 14
Antestia Shield Bug **41**
Antestiopsis orbitalis **41**
Anthomyia Fly **23**
Antlion **126, 129, 130**
Antlion larva **129**
Antlion pit sand trap **129**
Ants 60, **64**
Aphididae 46
Aphids 46, **47**

Apidae 69
Apis mellifera **69**
Aprocrita 60
Aptera fusca 177
Archibracon servillei **79**
Asarkina africana **28**
Asilidae 24
Aspidimorpha tecta **106**
Assassin Bug **39, 44**
Athene definita definita **92**
Australian Bug **47**

B

Bagworm larva **93**
Bagworms **93**
ballooning 94
barbed sting 70
Bark Mantid **55, 58**
Bark Shield Bug **41**
bed bug 39
bee bread 68
Bee Flies **32**
beehives 66
bee-mimicking **28**
Bees 60, 66
beeswax 61
Beetles 104
Belenois sp. **88**
bellows 185
Belonogaster sp. **71**
Belonogaster wasp **73**
Belostomatidae 179
Belted Fruit Chafer **118**
Bembix sp. **77**
Bittacus sp. **173**
Black and yellow Garden Fruit Chafer **117**
Black Fly 21
Bladder Grasshoppers 178
Blatta orientalis **162**
Blattodea 160
Blister Beetles **120**

Blow Fly 29, **30**
Blue Emperor Dragonfly 177
Bluebottles 29
Bluetail Damselflies **158**
Bombardier Beetles 125
Bombyliidae **32**
Brachinus spp. 125
Brachymeria kassalensis 78, **79**
Braconid sp. **78**
Braconid wasp **78**
Braconidae 78
breathing organs 15
Brenton Blue 81
Broad-bordered Grass Yellow **88**
Bromophila caffera **22**
Brown Locust 137, 139
Brown Longhorn Beetle **111**
Brown Shield Bug **42**
Brown-veined White **88**
Brush-footed Butterflies 91
Bunaea alcinoe **101**
Burrowing Grasshopper **141**
Butterflies 80, 83

C

Cabbage-tree Emperor Moth **101**
Cacyreus marshalli **92**
Caelifera 135
Calidea dregii **44**
Calliodes pretiosissima **94**
Calliphoridae 29
Calopterygidae 154
cantharadin 120
Cape Bluet 18
Cape Zebra Cockroach 160
Carabidae 125
Carebara vidua **66**
Carlisis wahlbergi **49**
Carpenter Bee **68**, 179
Carrion Beetle **106**
Caterpillars 100
Cave Crickets 135
Cerambycidae 110
Ceratitis capitata **31**
Ceratitis sp. **31**

Cercopidae **52**
Ceres Stream Damselfly 18
Ceriana **23**
Ceroplesis sp. **111**
Cetoniinae 117
Chalcidid wasps **79**
Chalcididae 78
Cheilomenes lunata **114**
chitin 15
Chlorocyphidae 154
chrysalis **85**, **87**
Chrysemosa sp. **128**
Chrysididae 76, **78**
Chrysomya marginalis **30**
Chrysoperla sp. **127**
Chrysopidae 127
Cicadellidae **51**
Cimicidae 39
Circellium baccus 180
Citrus Swallowtail **80**, **83**
Clear-wing Moths **98**
CMR beetle **107**, **120**
Coccinellidae 112
Cockroaches **160**
cocoon 15
Coenomorpha sp. **41**
Coleoptera 104
colour fringing 187
Common Hairtail butterfly **92**
compound eye 13
Condylostylus sp. **23**
Cone-headed Mantid **57**, **59**
Coreidae 48
Cottony Cushion Scale 47
Crab Spider **171**, **174**
Crane Fly **22**
Cream-striped Owl Moth **94**
cricket cages 138
Crickets 134, 145
Crimson-speckled Footman **95**
cryptically patterned **55**
Cryptocephalus decemnotatus **104**
Cuckoo Bees **67**
Cuckoo Wasp 76, **78**
cuckoo-spit 52

Culex Mosquito **36**
Culex sp. **37**
Culicidae 35
Curculionidae 119
Curcurbit Ladybird **116**
Cybister tripunctatus **122**
Cyligramma latona **94**
Cynthia cardui **17**, **90**
Cyphonistes vallatus **107**

D

Dalsira costalis **42**
Damselflies 152, 157
Danaus chrysippus **91**
Daphnis nerii **96**
Darkling Beetles **121**
Dejeania bombylans 178
Delta emarginatum **75**
Delta lepeleterii **76**
depth-of-field 190
Devonian age 18
Dicronorrhina derbyana **117**
Dictyophorus spumans **145**
digestive system 15
digital camera 173, 183
Dinogamasus 69
Diopsidae **34**
diopters 186
Diptera 20
Dolichopodidae **23**
Dorylus helvolus **66**
Dotted Border butterfly **88**
Dragonflies 152, **154**
Drone Fly **28**
dropwings 154
dung balls 109
Dung Beetles **108**
Dynastinae 107
Dytiscidae 122

E

egg sac **48**
Elegant Grasshopper **136**, **137**, **144**
elytra 14, 104, 123
Emperor Moth 179

Empusidae **59**
Enseferia 135
enzymes 25
Ephemeroptera 170
Eristalinus taeniops **28**
Eumenidae 74, **76**
Eurema brigitta brigitta **88**
Eurema sp. **88**
Eurytomidae 71
Exochomus flavipes **105**
exoskeleton 15
exposure 189
extension tubes 185, 187
eye span 34
eyespot **102**

F

femur 14
Fig Tree Borer Longhorn Beetle **112**
Fig Wasps 76
Fig-tree Moth **99**, **100**
filiform antennae 135
Flesh Flies **33**
Flies 20
Flower Flies 26
flying ants 164
Foam Grasshoppers 143
fontanelle 168
Fool's Gold Beetle **106**
Fork-horned Rhino Beetle **107**
formic acid 125
frenulum 83
Fruit Chafer **105**
Fruit Chafer Beetles **117**
Fruit Chafer larva **119**
Fruit Flies **31**
Fulgoridae **53**
Fungus-growing Termite 178

G

Garden Acraea **86**
Garden Cricket **138**
Garden Locust **140**, **141**
Garetta sp. **109**
Gargoyle Mantid **59**

Geranium Bronze butterfly **92**
Giant Antlion 180
Giant Dragonfly 177
Giant Dung Beetle 180
Giant Preying Mantis 179
Giant Table Mountain Cockroach 177
Giant Water Bugs 179
global warming phenomenon 171
Glymmatophora sp. **45**
Golden Plusia **99**
Golden-eyed Flies **127**
Grass Mantid **57**
Grass Stick Insect **173**
Grass Yellow Butterfly **88**
Grasshoppers **134**
Green Lacewing **127**
Green Mantid 55, **56**, 179
Green Vegetable Bug **42**
Greenbottles 29
Gregarious Antlion **126**, **132**
Grey Lacewing **128**
griffenflies 152
Gromphadorhina portentosa 161
Ground Beetles **125**
Gryllotalpa africana **147**
Gryllotalpidae **147**
Gryllus bimaculatus **138**
gymnosperms 19

H

Hagenomyia tristis **126**, **132**
Hairy Darkling Beetle **121**
halteres 14, 20
hamuli 61
Hangingfly **173**
Harvester Termite workers **164**
Harvester termites 169
Hawk Moth caterpillar **102**
Hawk Moths **96**
head 14
heart 15
Hedgehog Fly 178
Heleocopris andersoni 180
Heliocopris **108**
Heliocopris sp. **109**

hemimetabolous metamorphosis 15, 39
Hemiptera 38
Hermetia illucens **22**
hesperiidae 88
Heteroptera 38
Himatismus villosus **121**
Hippodamia variegata **113**
Hippotion celerio **96**
Hodotermes mossambicus **166**
holometabolous metamorphosis 15
Homoeoceris sp. **49**
Homoptera 38
honey 61, 66
Honey Bees **69**, **70**
honeydew **47**, 51, **64**
Hooked-winged Net-winged Beetle **124**
House Fly **22**, 23
Hover Flies **26**
Hyalites eponina **87**
Hymenoptera **60**

I

Icerya purchasi **47**
Ichneumonidae **60**, 78
Idolomorpha dentifrons **57**
imago 15, 170
Imbrasia belina 179
insect photography 181
insect spotting 171
insect wings 19
Ischnomantis fatilogua 179
Ischnura sp. **158**
Isoptera 164

J

jet propulsion 157
Jewel Beetles **44**
jugum 83
Julia Skimmer dragonflies **154**, **155**
Jumping Spider **172**, **181**
Junonia hierta **89**

K

Karoo Basin 19
Katydids 10, 145, **149**, **151**

King Cricket 145, **146**
King Monkey Moth **176**
Koppie Foam Grasshopper **135, 145**

L

labium 39
Lacewing larva **128**
Lacewings 126, **127**
Ladybird larva **115, 116**
Ladybird pupae **116**
Ladybirds 112, **113**
Lagria vulnerata **121**
lamellate antenna **109**
Lantern Bugs **53**
Lauxaniidae **22**
Leaf Katydid **150**
Leaf Mantid **59**
Leaf-footed Bugs **48**
Leafhoppers **51**
leaf-like 54
Lentulidae **143**
Lepidoptera 80
Lethocerus sp. **179**
Leucocelis amethystina 11, **107, 118**
Leucocelis sp. **105**
Libanasidus vittatus 145, **146**
light trap 176
Locustana pardalina 137
Locusts 134
Long-horn Beetles **110**
Long-horned Grasshoppers 135
Lunate Ladybird **114**
Lycaenidae **92**
Lycidae 123
Lycus melanurus **124**
Lycus sp. **123**

M

macro mode 183, 185
Macroglossum trochilus **96**
macrophotography 187
Macrotermes sp. **178**
Macrotoma sp. **111**
Madagascan Hissing Cockroach 161

maggot therapy 29
maggots **30**
Mantidflies **133**
Mantids **54**
Mantispidae 133
Mantodea **54**
March Bluetail Damselfly **173**
marginal feeding 174
Margodidae **47**
mask 153
Mason Wasp **62**
Mayfly **170**
Mecoptera 173
Mediterranean Fruit Fly **31**
Megalotheca longiceps 135
Meganeuropsis permiana 152
megapixels 183
Meloidae 120
Membracidae **49**
Metallic Assassin Bug **45**
Metallic Longhorn Beetle **111**
metamorphosis 15
milkweed 143
Milkweed Butterflies **91**
Milkweed Locust **145**
mites **165, 175, 176**
Mole Cricket 135, 138, **147, 148**
Molteno Formation 19
Mopane Worm 179
Mosquito 17, 35, **36**
Mosquito larvae **36**
Moth Flies **33**
Moth Lacewings **128**
Moths 80, 93
moulting 15
mouthparts 13, 14
Mud Dauber Wasp **76**
Mud Wasps **76**
Mulberry Hawk Moth **96**
Mutillidae 63
Mylabris oculata **107, 120**
Mylothris sp. **88**
Myrmeleontidae 129
Myrmicinae Ant **64**

N

naiad **153**
Naroma varipes **99, 100**
Nasidius Cricket **138**
Nasidius sp. **138**
nasus 168
Nephrotoma sp. **22**
Net-winged Beetles **123**
Neuroptera 126
Nezara viridula **42**
Nightshade Ladybird 116
Noctuidae 94, 99, 100
Northern Harvester Termite **166, 167**
notum 13
Nymphalidae 83, 86, 89, 90, 91
nymphs 15, 39

O

ocelli 14
Odonata 152
Oecanthus capensis 138
Oleander Hawk Moth **96**
ootheca 59, 161, **162**
Orachrysops niobe 81
Orange Dogs 83, **85**
Oriental Cockroach **162**
Orthetrum julia **155**
Orthoptera 134
osmeterium **85**
ovipositor 31, **138, 146**
Owl Moths **94**
Oxyhaloa sp. **162**
Oxyrachis sp. **50**

P

Pachnoda sinuata **117**
Painted Lady **90**
Palpares immensus 180
Palpares sp. **131, 132**
palps **147**
Paper wasps 71, **74**
Papilio demodocus **80, 83**
Papilionidae 83
Paralentula sp. **143**
parasitic mites 105

parasitic wasps 71, 78
Parktown Prawn 145, **146**
parthogenesis 39
Pedinorrhina sp. **118**
Pegesimallus sp. **24**
Pentatomidae **40**
Periplaneta americana **161, 163**
Phaneroptera sp. **150**
Phasmatodea 173
pheromones 14, 63
Phoracantha Longhorn **110**
Phoracantha sp. **110**
photomacrography 187
photomicrography 187
Phryneta spinator **105, 112**
Phyllocrania paradoxa **59**
Phymateus morbillosus **145**
Pieridae 87
plant-sucking bugs 38
Platycnemidae 154
Platystomatidae 21, **22**
Plume Moths **94, 95**
Pneumoridae 178
Polistes sp. **74**
Pondo-Pondo Longhorn Beetle **111**
Potato Ladybird 116
Potter Wasps 74, **75**
Praying Mantis **56**
Predacious Black Mealy Bug **105**
Predacious Water Beetles **122**
pretarsus 13
proboscis 17
prolegs 15
Promeces longipes **111**
Pseudoclanis postica **96**
Psorodes tuberculata **121**
Psychidae **93**
Psychodidae **33**
Psychopsidae **128**
Ptecticus elongatus **23, 185**
pteridophytes 19
Pterophoridae 94
pupa 15
Pyrgomantis rhodesica **57**
Pyrgomorphidae 137, 143

Q
queen ant 65

R
Rainbow Shield Bug **44**
raptorial forelegs 54, 133
Red Driver Ant **66**
Red Spider Mites **176**
Red-spotted Spittle Bug **39**
Reduviidae **44**
Red-veined Dropwing dragonfly **155**
Regal Blow Fly **30**
reversed 50 mm 187
Robber Fly **20, 24,** 178
Rock Fly **22**
Rodolia cardinalis 112
Roodepoort Copper Butterfly 81, 173
Rooibaadjie **135**
rostrum 14, 39
rysmiere 164

S
Salticidae sp. **172, 181**
Samaroblatta parvula **18**
Sand Wasp **76, 77**
sandfly 17
Sarcophagidae **33**
Scarabaeidae 108
scarabs 109
Sceliphron spirifex **76**
Scutelleridae 43
scutellum 44
Scuttle Fly **22**
segments 14
sesiidae 98
Shield Bug nymphs **43**
Shield Bugs **40**
Shield-backed Bugs 43, **44**
Short-horned Grasshoppers 135, **139**
sickle-shaped mandibles **129**
Silver-striped Hawk Moth **96**
single lens reflex camera 185
Skippers **88**
Snout Weevil **119**

social insects 63
social wasps 71
Soldier Fly **23, 185**
Solenostethium lilligerum **44**
solitary bees 66
solitary wasps 71
South Africa's Big 12 insects 177
sperm receptacle 158
Sphingidae 96, 102
Sphinx Moths **96**
Sphodromantis gastrica **56,** 179
spined forelegs **54**
spines 13
spiracles 13, 15
Spittle Bugs **52**
Spotted Amber Ladybird **113, 116**
Stable Flies **22**
stacking 186
Stalk-eyed Flies **34**
Stick Grasshopper **135,** 139, **140, 142**
Stick Insects 180
sting 61
Stinging caterpillars 103
Stink Bug **38, 40**
stridulation 137, 151
subimago 170
Sunflower Seed Bug **42**
supplementary lenses 186
swarm intelligence 165
sword-like antennae 135
Symphyta 60
Syrphid Fly **23**
syrphidae **26**

T
Table Mountain Cockroach 160
Tachinid Flies **34,** 178
Tachinidae **34**
Tapering Darkling Beetle **121**
tarsus 13, 14, **146**
taxonomy 12
tegmina 135
tele-extenders 185
Tenebrionidae 121
Ten-spotted Leaf Beetle **104**

Tephritidae **31**
termite mounds 165, 166, **168**
termite nest **168**
Termite nymphs **168**
Termite soldiers 165
Termites 164
Tetranychus urticae **176**
Tettigoniidae 149
Thanatophilus mutilatus **106**
Thermometer Cricket **148**
Thermophilum fornasinii **125**
Thomisidae sp. **171**, **174**
thorax 13, 14
thorn-like **50**
Thread-waisted Wasp **77**
tibia 13, 14
Toktokkie **121**
Torymidae 76
Tragocephala sp. **111**
Tree Cricket 138, **148**
Treehoppers 49, **50**
Triassic period 19
Triassoneura heidiae 18
Triatominae 44
Tricarinodynerus sp. **75**
Trichoplusia orichalcea **99**
Trithemis annulata **152**, **157**
Trithemis arteriosa **155**
True Bugs 38
True Leaf Katydid **149**
Tsetse Fly 17, 21
Twig Snout Bugs **53**
Twig Wilter Bugs **48**, **55**
tympanal 151
tympanic organs 138

U
Utetheisa pulchella **95**

V
Vanessa cardui **90**
Veld Antlion **131**
velvet ants 63
Vespidae 61, **71**
Violet Dropwing dragonfly **152**, **157**

W
Wandering Glider **155**
Wasps 60, 71
Wattle Bagworm 93
Wavy Owl Moth **94**
Weevils **119**
white ants 164
wild cockroaches **161**
Wild Honey Bees 69
Window-waisted Fly **22**
Wingless Grasshoppers **143**
wings 14
worker ant **65**

X
Xylocopa sp. **68**, 179
Xylocopinae 68

Y
Yellow and Black Banded Lily Borer **100**
Yellow Pansy **89**

Z
Zabalius aridus **149**
Zig-zag Fruit Chafer **106**, **117**, **118**
Zonocerus elegans **136**
Zygoptera 153, **159**